The Quest for Oil

W. G. ROBERTS

The Quest for Oil

ILLUSTRATED WITH PHOTOGRAPHS AND DIAGRAMS

S. G. PHILLIPS ⚡ New York

Library of Congress Cataloging in Publication Data

Roberts, William Geoffrey.
  The quest for oil.

  (The World we are making)
  Includes index.
  SUMMARY: A survey of the oil industry discussing
how and where oil is found, the way fuels are
produced and used, and the many products derived from oil.
      1. Petroleum engineering—Juvenile literature.
[1. Petroleum.   2. Petroleum industry and trade]
I. Title.
TN870.3.R6   1977   338.2'7'282   76-54736
ISBN 0-87599-225-0

Contents

List of Illustrations

LINE DRAWINGS AND DIAGRAMS

Acknowledgments

Author and publisher gratefully acknowledge help received, and permission to reproduce illustration material from the following:

British Petroleum Company Ltd (Figs. 2–6, photos nos. 3, 4, 6–8, 10, 11, 13–15, 19, 20, 23, 29, 31, 32)

Esso Petroleum Ltd (photos nos. 5, 16–18, 21, 24, 28, 33)

Keystone Press Agency (photo no. 22)

Radio Times Hulton Picture Library (Fig. 1)

Shell International Petroleum Company Ltd (photos nos. 2, 12, 25–27, 30)

United States Information Service (photo no. 1)

The Port of New York Authority (photo no. 9)

Introduction

This book first appeared in Britain, which is part-way through changing to the Metric system of measurement. Accordingly, metric units appear throughout. Since metric units are used by scientists all over the world, and are gradually being adopted for everyday use in most countries which do not already have them, we have thought it best to stay with the metric system and add the following simple conversion notes. The factors quoted do not give precise equivalents in every case; they are intended as a simple guide, accurate enough for everyday conversions into the more familiar units.

Measure of:	*Metric*	*Traditional*
Length	1 metre	3.3 feet
	1 kilometre	5/8 mile
	25 millimetres	1 inch
Area	1 hectare	2½ acres
Volume	1 litre	¼ gallon (US)
	160 litres	* 1 barrel (42 US gallons)
Mass	1 kilogram	2.2 pounds
	1 metric ton	1.1 short tons (US)
Pressure	1 bar	15 pounds per square inch
Power	1 kilowatt	¾ horse-power
Temperature	0° C	32°F (exactly)
	100°C	212°F (exactly)

To convert any other temperature to °F, multiply the °C by 1.8 and *add* 32.

* The oil industry often uses barrels as a measure of liquid volume for ships and tanks, and to describe the daily throughput of refinery processes. Conversion from volume to mass depends on the density of the oil in question, but as a *very* rough guide, 1 ton = 7½ barrels (this is strictly accurate only for an oil of relative density 0.84).

1 · Fuels and Energy

The months of preparation are over. All systems have been checked and the countdown is nearly complete. In a few seconds another rocket will blast off on its way to the moon. A new triumph of engineering, electronics and sheer human perseverance is about to take men on a journey which has been dreamed of for centuries.

The first stage of the American Saturn 5 rocket was designed to be propelled by kerosene—a fuel derived from crude oil. Why kerosene? Because it is a well-proven fuel, backed by the vast experience of the oil and aircraft industries. It is cheap, and it is readily available in the 1,000-ton quantities needed for the job. The second and third stages of this type of rocket use special high-energy fuels, because although smaller quantities are then needed, the amount of weight to be carried becomes vital. Without a product of the oil industry, however, the Apollo project would—literally—never have got off the ground.

Space travel is just the latest, and perhaps the most

1 *Blast-off of an American moon rocket;*
   the first stage is propelled by kerosene

spectacular, use of products from an industry which has been growing up for barely one hundred years. Kerosene was in fact the very beginning of the oil industry, because it was needed for oil lamps. Its latest job would have staggered the imagination of the oil pioneers of the mid-nineteenth century. This book looks at the development of the industry, and the complex technology which sustains it.

Oil has been described as 'black gold' and 'the lifeblood of industry'. These vivid, if slightly flowery phrases have a real meaning. More oil and gas are produced in the world each year than any other single commodity; more money is involved than in any other industry; every other industry depends on oil in some form for part of its operations. Oil is of enormous value to the countries where it is produced from the ground; so much so that the less developed countries sometimes simply do not know what to do with their newfound wealth. It is said that until very recently the ruler of one small state on the Arabian Gulf used to keep his revenues, amounting to millions of pounds, in a box in his bedroom; he preferred gold, but banknotes were also acceptable. And there the money stayed—unused.

To see why oil is so important, it is necessary to understand what oil is worth in terms of other fuels, and what properties make oil so attractive.

Since the dawn of history, people have needed fuel, first of all simply for personal warmth and cooking, later for the heat processes which are the basis of almost all industry.

The first fuel was wood, and it went unchallenged for thousands of years simply because it was readily available. One of the earliest discoveries was that by slow heating without allowing the access of air, wood could be turned into charcoal. Charcoal in its turn could be burnt to give a stronger heat which was sufficient for the extraction and working of metals. The use of metals, along with the more effective use of fuels, has been the mainstay of all modern industrial development. Wood and charcoal held their own until about the sixteenth century, when it was realized that supplies of wood were running short, and that the material would in any case be better used for building houses and ships than for burning.

Fortunately, there was another fuel available—coal. It is found in many places all over the world, but its large-scale use was pioneered in Europe. By the eighteenth century it was to be the main foundation of the Industrial Revolution. It was soon clear that coal was a much better fuel than wood both for domestic and industrial use. This was especially true for the working of metals and for raising steam for driving machinery. The use of steam gave man power on a scale which he had never known before.

Once the use of steam, raised by coal fires, had been established, it was not long before the boilers and the machines using the steam were made safer, lighter and more efficient. Steam-engines were made for the tramways at the mines, and very soon railways sprang from this development. It was some years before steam-engines could be made sufficiently reliable for ships to dispense with sails completely, but man was at last free from total dependence on wind and animal power for transportation.

Coal is also the parent of two important secondary fuels. Coke is familiar as a fuel for household boilers, but it has far more important uses in industry, especially in the manufacture of iron and steel. Coal-gas was used, before electricity was generally available, for household lighting and heating, and is still widely used for the latter. More recently it has been used for industrial purposes where it is important to have a clean, easily controlled flame, and in factories where it is not necessary to keep large boilers and furnaces running continuously.

In the first half of the nineteenth century, scientists under the lead of men like Michael Faraday were experimenting with electricity. It was some time before this source of power could be used universally, partly because it is a secondary form of energy. This means that it is most usually made by providing heat to raise steam, using the steam to provide mechanical energy, and then converting the mechanical energy to electricity. Only very recently has it been possible to simplify this cycle and eliminate the mechanical devices such as turbines and dynamos. This can be done by means of the 'fuel cell', but this type of apparatus is still in the experimental stage. The conventional power station must continue to rely on raising steam, feeding this to a turbine, which in turn drives a generator. Electricity, even when made in the most efficient modern stations, is a relatively expensive form of energy.

Electricity can also be generated using water power. Water-driven mills have an ancient history, but water is nowadays used on a large scale only for electrical plant. Even then, it can only be used where the accidents of geography—a mountainous region, for example—enable us to trap large quantities of water in dams, make it run downhill to convert its potential energy into kinetic or moving energy, and thus drive a special type of turbine.

Such plants exist in many parts of the world, and are often of very large capacity, but they still account for only a small portion of the world's total electrical needs. A very special kind of hydro-electric station uses the rise and fall of the tide in narrow estuaries to drive turbines, but suitable places for such stations are quite rare.

The winds have gone out of favour as a source of power, since they are too unreliable. However, in suitable places it is still possible to find small wind-driven generators providing a domestic electric supply.

Nuclear, or atomic, energy is now harnessed to raise steam and drive turbines to generate electricity. Nuclear power stations are very expensive to build, but relatively cheap to run, and will certainly be an increasingly important way of satisfying the world's power needs. Aside from cost, there are two major problems barring the way to quick expansion. Firstly, it is essential to ensure that the nuclear reactors are safe from the possibility of explosion or leakage of radioactive material. The risk is already quite low, but not sufficiently so to allow stations to be sited near built-up areas. Secondly, the difficulties of disposal of radioactive waste must be overcome, since it can be dangerous for hundreds of years. There is no quick and cheap solution to either problem.

The use of solar energy is now being considered seriously as a means of conserving conventional fuels and preventing pollution. Obviously, solar energy is of most use in areas where there is plenty of sunshine. Even there, however, it is still necessary to have conventional power plant to provide for night use and the occasional dull or wet period. Anything more than partial use of this "free fuel" must wait until the problem of large-scale storage of electric power can be solved.

2 · The Beginnings of the Oil Industry

The first oils to be used by man were not of mineral origin at all, but came from vegetable and animal sources. These have been, and still are, used for simple lamps and stoves, as lubricants for slow-moving machinery, as the basis of perfumes, and for foods.

The first known deposits of mineral oil, or petroleum, were found because they showed themselves as seepages from underground reservoirs. They were mostly of two kinds—natural 'lakes' of bitumen like those in Trinidad and at La Brea in California, and leaks of natural gas such as gave rise to the Perpetual Fires near Mosul in Iraq. In some places there were small seepages of a dark, moderately viscous or thick liquid which was what we now know as crude oil. Limited uses for these petroleum deposits have been known for thousands of years—Noah's Ark was caulked with pitch ('Make thee an ark . . . pitch it within and without with pitch')—and it was also known that these oils were inflammable, though burning them in primitive lamps must have been

16

a dirty and smelly business. Where crude oil was extracted from the ground at all, it was usual to dig a deep pit in a seepage area and allow the pit to fill slowly until there was enough to bail it out with buckets. This method was actually used in Burma and China hundreds of years ago. It was also found, about the middle of the nineteenth century, that a crude oil could be made by heating to high temperatures certain kinds of oily shale which look rather like coal but have a very high proportion of ash-forming, rock-like material and are not suitable for burning raw.

The first big step towards the establishment of an oil industry was the discovery, around 1850, that a much improved burning oil could be made by distilling crude oil in the same way that whisky and brandy and other spirits for drinking had been made for many years. This discovery greatly increased the demand for petroleum oil for burning in lamps.

The next step was to get it from the ground by drilling wells, as one might for water. The credit for drilling the first mineral oil well is usually given to one Colonel Drake, who drilled a 70-foot well near Titusville in Pennsylvania in 1859. Colonel Drake and the company who employed him started something of which the later growth cannot have been guessed at, either by themselves or by the thousands of men who were to try the same sort of operation over the next few years.

In the early days of the modern industry, virtually the only use for crude oil was to make the distilled product called kerosene or paraffin. It was used for oil lamps and stoves, and most of the light spirit and the residue from distillation was burnt to waste or thrown away. Before long, some of this waste oil found uses—the light spirit as a solvent for various manufacturing processes and the high boiling part as a basis for lubricating oil manufacture. Towards the end of the

Fig. 1 *Petroleum oilworks, Pennsylvania*

nineteenth century, the first motor cars began to appear on the roads, and the light spirit came into its own as a fuel for these machines.

Means were developed for burning the thick residual fuel oil under boilers on land and in ships in place of coal. Very thick residues began to be used as a substitute for natural pitch and coal tar in jobs where waterproofing qualities were needed, notably in road surfacing. It was found that wax could be extracted from the part of the oil used for lubricant manufacture, and the lubricating oil was improved at the same time. Wax was mainly in demand for making candles at that time, but many other uses have been developed since, including the coating of paper and cardboard to make it water-resistant.

The first companies in the petroleum industry were very

small concerns compared with the giant companies of today. There was intense rivalry and competition, and the weaker companies were apt to go out of business very suddenly. The better-run or more ruthless firms prospered and grew rapidly. Sometimes they grew too big. This happened to Standard Oil in the United States, and when its commercial power became too great the company was broken up into smaller independent parts by the law courts. The parts continued as highly successful businesses, and one of them—Standard Oil of New Jersey—has become by legal means the largest of the world's giant oil companies.

The story of Shell is almost as successful, and rather less chequered. It started as a small general trading company which branched out into oil in the 1890's. Shell's rapid rise among the big oil firms really began when it joined with the Royal Dutch Company in 1907. The other large companies, including Gulf, Texaco, Mobil, Chevron and British Petroleum (BP), were all started strictly for oil business. Each has concentrated on this task or closely related chemical manufacturing ever since, with only small and unimportant excursions into other activities. All of today's great oil firms had very modest beginnings, even the largest have been through difficult times when failure was a very real possibility. Competition has seldom slackened, and the most efficient firms have achieved their position because of the growing need for their products.

The number of uses for oil products, and the total demand for oil, has grown at an ever-increasing rate since the beginning of the twentieth century. The most obvious areas of expansion have been in fuels for road vehicles and aircraft, and demands for other types of product have also grown beyond recognition. Not only has the demand for quantity increased, but the quality offered has also steadily improved.

To keep pace with the increase in quantity of oil needed by all kinds of domestic and industrial users, the industry has had to improve its own means of manufacture, transportation and marketing. Ocean transport of oil started with the carriage of a few tons of oil in wooden barrels on sailing ships; today, the larger tankers carry about 500,000 tons of crude oil at a time, and it is possible that within a few years ships will be built to carry even larger quantities as a single cargo.

Enormous progress has also been made in the equipment used for finding the places where oil is likely to occur, and extracting it from the ground. In the early days they found oil by observing surface seepages and then sinking a fairly shallow well. Nowadays all the resources of modern geology are employed to establish where oil might have been formed, and advances in drilling techniques enable us to drill holes down to depths of four or five miles should this prove necessary.

Any introduction to the subject of oil would be incomplete without at least a brief mention of natural gas. This fuel is closely related to crude oil, it is often found in the same places as oil, and much of the exploration and production work is undertaken by oil companies. Natural gas was first exploited on a large scale in the United States, and it is there that more use is made of it than anywhere else at present. However, gas is found in most of the other oil-producing areas, and is now in commercial production in the Middle East, North Africa, Pakistan, New Zealand, France, Italy, Holland, Russia, and from under the North Sea. Some of these areas do not have crude oil in noticeable quantities; in others crude oil is the major product and gas is a side-line for the present. The total amounts of gas available are enormous, and besides offering a new form of fuel in many

2 'Christmas tree' on a gas well head, New Zealand

countries, natural gas has largely replaced coal gas in countries such as Britain within a matter of years.

Energy can be measured in various ways—by work done, expressed in horsepower, or by its equivalent in heating effect, measured in British Thermal Units (Btu) or in calories. One Btu is roughly equal to one kilojoule. In the case of electricity, the energy is usually expressed as kilo-watt-hours (kwh), which are the 'units' which appear on one's household electricity bill. Each of these types of energy unit is scientifically sound, but none of them is very convenient for statements about very large amounts of energy such as are involved in the world's total energy needs. Nor is it particularly easy to do the mental arithmetic necessary to compare the demands for different types of energy.

What is needed is a measure in terms of one commonly used fuel which can be burnt to release a known amount of energy. Because coal was for many years the most widely used fuel, it has become conventional to turn all national and global energy demands into the Hard Coal Equivalent, measured in tons. Once we know that burning one pound of standard hard coal releases 12,000 Btu, it is not difficult to convert other fuels to this equivalent. One pound of oil gives about 18,000 Btu, one cubic foot of natural gas gives about 1,000 Btu, and coal gas is commonly standardised at 500 Btu per cubic foot. One unit of electrical energy, completely converted to heat, gives 3,400 Btu. So, one ton of hard coal is equivalent to roughly: 0.67 tons of oil, or 7,900 kwh of electricity, or 27,000 cubic feet of natural gas.

Knowing this, tables can show the amounts of energy needed in the whole world, or parts of it, according to the source of the primary fuel used. The units will all be the same—tons of Hard Coal Equivalent. In the following table the units are *millions* of tons of Hard Coal Equivalent:

AREA	YEAR	COAL	OIL	NATURAL GAS	HYDRO-ELEC. & NUCLEAR	TOTAL
N. America	1965	487	906	681	125	2199
	1970	534	1151	895	170	2750
	1975	538	1270	841	276	2925
W. Europe	1965	541	583	30	125	1279
	1970	478	938	113	152	1681
	1975	369	997	231	184	1781
World	1965	2545	2294	970	372	6181
	1970	2699	3412	1432	494	8037
	1975	2833	4053	1662	684	9232

These figures are only approximate, but they give an idea of the size of the world's primary fuel needs. Notice three things in particular about the table. Firstly, world demand for primary fuel grew rapidly up to 1973, oil and gas averaging 7 percent per year. After a sudden halt the rate is picking up again. Secondly, well over half the fuel is used in the industrial countries of Western Europe and North America, which between them have less than a quarter of the world's population. Thirdly, electricity is included in the figure for the primary fuel used in its generation, and the figures for coal include coke and coal gas. Town gas and electricity supplies for most countries in Western Europe are dependent largely on coal. In the United States the picture is different, and although coal is still important, natural gas has for the past twenty years been the primary source for two-thirds of total gas and electricity consumed.

By 1960, over half the world's energy needs were being met by oil and natural gas. In 1968 the share was growing, and in that year, for the first time, the world's markets absorbed over 2,000 million tons of crude oil. By 1975 the figure was close to 2.75 billion tons.

Oil and natural gas both occur in nature, and have been known for thousands of years, but neither fuel had significant commercial use until about one hundred years ago. Demand for fuels in general and oil in particular will most certainly continue to grow, and as this happens, more and more of the world's population will feel the effects of the industrial revolution which began in Europe 200 years ago.

In addition to its uses for fuel and lubricants, we now use products of the oil industry to make our clothing and to build and furnish our houses. We already have ways of turning oil into a protein concentrate which can be used to supplement animal feedstuffs, and the next step may well be for humans to eat oil products as well. Nothing that has happened in the industry in the past hundred years suggests that our scope for inventiveness is by any means exhausted, so even more remarkable things may happen in the next hundred.

3 · Looking for Oil

In order to supply the 2700 million tons of oil needed every year to help satisfy the modern world's demands, it is necessary first to find where the oil is hidden in the ground, and then to bring it to the surface. How then is crude oil formed, and why does it become trapped in the ground?

A number of theories have been put forward to account for the existence of crude oil. One theory is that oil could be formed by the interaction of volcanic gases before they reach the earth's surface. The necessary chemical reactions are possible at the very high temperatures and pressures that exist in the lower parts of the earth's crust. This might account for some of the crude oil found, at least in areas of volcanic activity. But it cannot account for all oil, because much is discovered in areas where there never have been volcanoes. It is generally accepted that most crude oil deposits were formed in a way similar in many respects to the formation of coal. It is not very difficult to show that coal consists of the remains of trees and plants which grew in

25

swampy ground and which later became buried under layers of mud and sand which hardened into rock. Pieces of woody material and other vegetable matter can be identified in coal to prove this, and the types of plant found are ones which could only have grown in warm damp conditions.

Oil is different in two ways. It appears not to have formed in swamps, but in parts of the sea which were gradually becoming deeper. The chemical and geological evidence also suggests that it consists of the partly decomposed and altered remains of fishes and small marine animals and plants, many of them of microscopic size. These remains supplied the raw material, including all the necessary carbon and hydrogen for the formation of oil. Anything suitable which sank to the bottom of the sea would find itself in an environment where there is little oxygen, and would not decompose completely as it would in places where air could get at it freely. Once the layer of remains of sea creatures was covered with further layers of mud and silt and sand, it would be put under even greater pressures which are capable of completing the conversion of once-living or organic matter to crude oil. Usually, the organic remains would be mixed with silt and with the bones and shells of such creatures as possessed them.

There is evidence that this sort of thing is still going on today at the bottom of parts of the oceans. The whole process of accumulating enough raw material to make thousands of millions of tons of oil takes a long time, time which must be measured in millions of years. All our oil deposits are found in rocks which may be even hundreds of millions of years old. It is also notable that oil is very rarely found except in rock which was formed under the sea by the deposition of layers of mud, sand and limestone. It is not found, for instance, in granite, or in the rocks formed by volcanic action. Oil is hardly ever found in the sediments formed below the shallow water of lakes, and not very often in the type of sandstone which is a relic of old deserts. When it is found in non-marine rocks, there is a special reason.

Since oil is liquid, and moreover is lighter than water, it may seem strange that it stays in the rock at all, and is not lost from the surface of the sea in which it formed, or lost by being pressed out of the rock at some later time. The reason is that these things do indeed happen, unless something else takes place to stop them. Oil may be lost before it can be trapped in the rock at all; it can also be forced to move from where it was formed into neighbouring rock, or even forced right out of the surface and lost. If oil is to be trapped in the ground, the first thing which must happen is that the layer of organic sediment on the sea floor must be covered by a layer of fine mud or silt through which liquids cannot pass. The retained organic matter can then be held in place while it is transformed into crude oil. The other important condition is that any later rock movements must take place in such a way that the oil remains trapped until someone drills a well and lets it out to the surface.

Oil can remain trapped in the depths of the earth in a variety of ways, which can best be described by diagrams. Oil is almost invariably found in rocks like sandstone and some kinds of limestone. The vital feature is that 'reservoir rock' is porous, that is, the rocks are not so solid as they might seem, but have free space between the grains, or show small fissures and splits in which the oil can accumulate and through which it can move.

In the slow passage of geological time—millions of years—enormous pressures can build up in the earth's crust, resulting in the folding and splitting of solid rock. When the folding is slow and relatively gentle, ridges and domes can be formed, and provided that the porous reservoir rock has a fine-grained non-porous 'cap rock' above it, liquids can be trapped in the dome. This is the simplest form of structure which may contain oil. There may be gas and water trapped as well, and in this case the light gas will eventually separate towards the top of the dome. Gas and oil which were formed some distance away may be forced into such a structure, provided there is pressure to move it and porous rock through which it can travel, however slowly.

Other important types of rock structure in which oil may be found are the fault trap, the stratigraphic trap, and the salt dome trap. The diagrams show the sections we should see if we could cut our way down several thousand feet into the earth along a straight line.

A fault is a break in the earth's crust, where the rock to one side has been pushed upwards (or downwards). Where porous rock on one side meets impermeable rock on the

Fig. 2   *Gas, oil and water are trapped in the dome, below the cap rock*

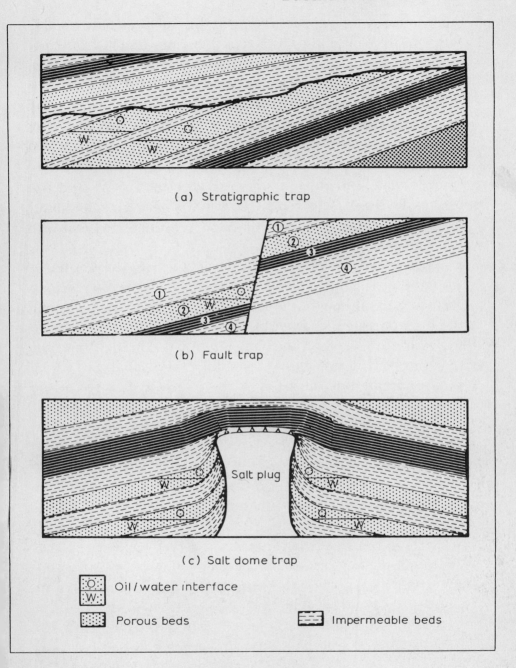

(a) Stratigraphic trap

(b) Fault trap

(c) Salt dome trap

Oil/water interface

Porous beds

Impermeable beds

Fig. 3 *Three forms of trap shown in cross section*

other, oil can be trapped along the line of the fault, as the impermeable, or non-porous rock prevents liquid from migrating upwards and being lost on the surface. Here, as in other forms of trap, the oil may arrive through the porous strata long after the trap structures have been formed, the oil having originally been formed some distance away.

A stratigraphic trap can be formed when a fold in the rocks has first been forced up above sea-level and been eroded away, and then submerged again and covered with further layers of sediment. If the lowest layer of the new sediment is impermeable, a reservoir is formed where oil can accumulate.

In some parts of the world, notably in the southern United States, large bodies of rock salt exist deep below the surface. Salt, although it is solid, flows relatively easily under the high pressures exerted by earth movements, and can be forced into a plug or dome. Oil cannot pass through the salt, so it can be trapped against the sides of the dome.

To find oil, one must first look for rock structures of the types just described, or other more complicated ones which are known from past experience to be possible oil traps. There is never any certainty that oil will be found, even in an ideal rock structure, but there is no point whatever in doing further work unless the right conditions for a trap can be shown to exist.

A skilled geologist can get a lot of information about possible oil-bearing structures simply from looking at maps which show how the rocks appear at the surface. But many areas which might be promising for oil exploration have no maps of any kind, let alone geological ones. In such a case the first thing is usually to arrange for an aerial photographic survey. An aeroplane flies on a set course, normally a series of parallel lines, taking photographs from a known height at carefully calculated intervals, until a large mosaic of pictures has been taken. Since we want to know the height of the ground at different points, and this is not possible to work out from a single photograph, successive pictures are taken which overlap by a known and constant amount. We then have two photographs of each area of ground, and by viewing these through a stereoscope we can get a three-dimensional effect and a good indication of the relative heights of adjoining bits of ground. Very careful flying is needed, and radio beacons are used wherever possible to help the pilot maintain an accurate course during his survey. All this will give the basis for a good conventional map, and often shows up surface rock patterns very clearly, especially in barren country.

The geologists then look at the map which has been built up and select areas for examination on the surface. Surface exploration can be very difficult in country which is covered with towns and villages, and farmland with little or no rock appearing at ground level. In mountainous or uninhabited country other difficulties arise because it may take a long time to get from place to place. In the past it was necessary to walk or use horses to get around such areas. Nowadays, motor transport may be used, and when the going gets too tough for cars and trucks the geologist can take to a helicopter, which can land him in almost any place which he may want to examine more closely.

On the ground the geologist looks at the type of rock, the direction and angle at which the rock beds slope, and takes samples for analysis and for identification of fossils which will indicate the age of the rock. Often the most useful fossils are of microscopic size, frequently they are quite small, and it is rare indeed to find things like dinosaur skeletons!

When the hard rock is covered by desert sand or arctic bog, or by the waters of the sea, a conventional map is not much help, and it may not be possible to make up a geological map from surface inspection. In any case the structures of real interest may be hidden at depth. There are three important ways of finding out about hidden rock. These can be compared to the use of X-rays by a surgeon who wants to examine the inside of a patient before he operates. More than one technique may have to be used, and the results supplement each other and the information obtained by geological surface surveys.

The first of these geophysical exploration methods is the gravimetric survey. Because the earth is not perfectly spherical, but has hills and valleys and oceans, and bulges slightly at the equator as well, and because rocks are not all equally dense, the pull of gravity varies very slightly from point to point. Oil is usually found in older rocks rather than in very recent ones, and older rocks tend to be more dense. Crystalline rocks like granite, in which oil is never found, are mostly extremely dense. Salt on the other hand is not very dense at all. So a rapid drop in readings on a gravimeter, which is the sensitive instrument used to detect these differences in gravitational pull, could indicate to the surveyor that he was passing over a salt dome. Such a change could also indicate the position of a fault in hidden rocks. The interpretation of a geophysical record is not easy; a similar record might mean two very different things, and a lot of experience is necessary to get useful and reliable answers.

The second geophysical survey technique depends on the fact that the earth is a huge magnet, whose poles lie near the geographical north and south poles. Locally, the strength and direction of the resulting magnetic field is affected by the nature of the rocks, since some of them are slightly magnetic. Rocks containing a lot of iron may be very magnetic, as you might expect. Maps which show the variation in magnetic field over an area can be produced, and will give some further information about the types of rock present beneath the surface. This kind of survey has the advantage that the magnetometer which is used to measure the magnetic variations can be mounted in an aircraft. The survey is then conducted by flying along prearranged lines as in photographic map-making.

There is another way of getting more information about hidden rocks, and this is perhaps the most spectacular of the three. The surveyor sets out to make his own very small private earthquakes. This is known as the seismic method of surveying. Earthquake waves can travel through rock for long distances; their speed of travel depends on the density of the rock. The waves can be reflected when they meet the boundary between rocks of different densities. They can also be refracted, or bent, when they pass across such boundaries. The laws governing the passage of earthquake or shock waves through solids are in fact similar to those which apply to light when it meets a glass surface in a lens or mirror. If we deliberately make a small earthquake and set out geophones and recording apparatus around the point where the shock waves start, we can find out how long it takes for the waves to reach various points. The waves the surveyor is mainly interested in are those which have passed down into the earth and then been turned so that they come back to the recording machinery.

To make a suitable earthquake, explosive charges are normally used, setting off perhaps 10 kg of dynamite in a shallow hole. The geophones may be laid out over distances of a few hundred yards. If a larger area is to be covered, a bigger explosive charge may be needed. When a small area is being examined and it is not necessary for the shock waves to reach great depths, they can be produced by dropping a very heavy weight. This is useful where explosives would be too dangerous or inconvenient. The records are usually taken on

3 *Seismic shot firing during survey operations*
  in the Rocky Mountains, Canada

fast-moving film. From the records it is possible to work out
much about the density of the sub-surface rocks, their
thicknesses, and how the strata relate to one another. The
information gained in this way is very complex, but use of
the electronic computer speeds up the calculations involved.

All these methods can be adapted for use in exploring the
shallower parts of the oceans, and many oil and gas fields
have been discovered in such areas, especially in the Gulf of
Mexico, around Arabia and Iran, off Australia and in the
North Sea.

When all this work has been finished by the geologists and geophysicists it is clear which are the places where it is possible that oil might be found, and which areas look unlikely. There is only one way of actually finding oil, and that is to make a hole in the ground and see whether there is anything at the bottom of it. We are now a long way from the Burmese oil pits or Colonel Drake's simple well, both of which were sunk in known seepage areas. The modern oil well may have to be many thousands of feet deep. The work requires large and elaborate equipment, and is extremely expensive. One hole in the ground could cost more than a million dollars and contribute nothing except some drilling experience and a small addition to geological knowledge. This is why so much exploration is essential before any drilling is started.

Because of the huge cost which may be involved in drilling, it is nowadays extremely rare to hear of anyone sinking a true 'wildcat' well—that is, one drilled simply because someone has a hunch that his patch of ground has oil beneath. It is even rarer to hear of such a venture succeeding, although the large 'Spindletop' field in Texas was found in this way. Indeed, only about one in ten of wells sunk in carefully explored country ever produce useful finds; the other nine find nothing except perhaps a small amount of gas or oil which is not worth collecting. Of course, once a productive well has been drilled in an area, the chances of success nearby are greatly improved.

In the early days of industry, and particularly in America where exploration and drilling were often carried out by very small groups of men working on small tracts of land, disputes over possession of oil were not infrequent. It was not too difficult, once a neighbour had discovered oil, to drill a bigger and better hole from one's own patch and drain out the oil which the other man had found. The process was made even simpler when the drillers found out how to drill at an angle so that the hole could actually finish up under the other man's land, possibly before he even noticed what was going on!

The best thing of course is to find a new field in a remote place and have wells drilled and producing over the largest area possible, before anyone else comes into the region. So people were always trying for oil in new and unlikely areas and there are many fields today in places where experts have been prepared to stake their professional reputations that no oil could ever be found. The discoveries of the past twenty or thirty years, however, have all followed painstaking surveys, designed to reduce the chances of complete failure once the drilling starts. Even so in new areas there may be many 'dry' holes before success is achieved.

4 · Getting Crude Oil from the Ground

Exploration gives the technical background for a decision on drilling. But before drilling can begin, and indeed usually before a survey can be undertaken, there are other matters to consider. The oil company proposing to start any operation must have permission from the government in whose territory it wishes to work, and must also come to some agreement with the owner (if any) of particular plots of land which may be disturbed. In most countries mineral rights belong to the government, and not to the owner of the ground under which the minerals lie. In previously unexplored country, it is common for the area to be split up into large slices, which may each be hundreds of square miles. These slices are known as concessions. Interested companies decide, on the basis of any geological information which may be available, which bits they would most like to have. They then make bids to the government for the privilege of exploring, the concession normally going to the highest bidder. It will probably be a condition of the concession that

at least one exploratory well must be drilled within a set space of time. Preliminary agreement may be included on payments to the host government for any oil that is found.

The geological structure of most of the more industrially advanced parts of the world, such as Europe and the United States, is fairly well known, and oil may already be in production if there is any to be found in a particular area. So, very often, new exploration has to be undertaken in the most inhospitable places, such as the deserts of the Middle East and North Africa, the arctic wastes of Russia, Alaska and Northern Canada, or under the shallower parts of the oceans on what we call the 'continental shelf.'

When serious oil exploration first started, and a remote area was to be examined, there was nothing for it but to camp out. This is of course great fun for a holiday in a reasonable climate. It is rather less fun if you have to do it for months on end in a jungle or a sweltering desert; when you have to go out every day, regardless of the weather, and then work in a tent at night by the light of an oil lamp, trying to keep records of all you have done.

Fortunately for us, the oil prospectors were hardy and determined men. Things are in some ways easier today, with transportable huts, and air-conditioned caravans for workers in really hot climates. But as less and less of the earth's surface remains unexplored, the last bits are likely to be the least pleasant to live and work in. The map-makers and geologists in the middle of the Sahara or in North Alaska deserve and need anything which can make their working and living quarters more comfortable. The men who do this sort of job still need to be tough, independent, and prepared to work far from city comforts for long periods, in addition to being masters of an increasingly technical profession.

The equipment and technique of drilling is much the same wherever the well is to be sunk. Most of today's work is

4   *Survey party's camp in the Canadian Rockies*

done with some form of rotary drill. The vital part of the drill is a rotating bit, made of very hard steel and fitted with teeth which may have small industrial diamonds set into them. The remainder of the rig is there to provide power to rotate the bit, to apply weight to make it bite into the rock, and to circulate fluid to keep the system cool and carry away rock particles from the bottom of the hole. The bit is carried at the lower end of a number of sections of steel pipe, each usually 10 metres long and fitted so that they can be screwed together in much the same way as the cane rods used in sweeping chimneys or clearing drains. The pipe sections just above the bit are called 'drill collars'. They are very heavy so as to put weight on the bit when the hole is started. They can be up to 300 mm in diameter, with only a 63 mm hole down the middle.

The remaining pipes are lighter, a common size being 114 mm outside diameter, with a wall thickness of 10 mm, so that the hole in the middle is 95 mm across. The uppermost pipe is square outside, and is made so that it can slide up and down through a square hole in a revolving platform known as the 'rotary table'. When the rotary table is turned, the square section of pipe or 'kelly' rotates with it, and the whole of the rest of the 'drill string' of pipes turns so as to drive the bit.

The fluid used to cool the bit and remove rock debris is a specially made up mud, which is pumped down the centre hole in the drill pipe and out through jets in the bit, returning to the surface through the wider section of the hole round the drill string. As the hole gets deeper, more lengths of drill pipe are screwed into the top end of the string, immediately below the kelly, which must of course be removed and replaced each time a new section is added.

The visible part of the drilling rig consists of engines to provide power, and equipment for utilising this power to

Fig. 4 *Diagram of a rotary drilling rig*

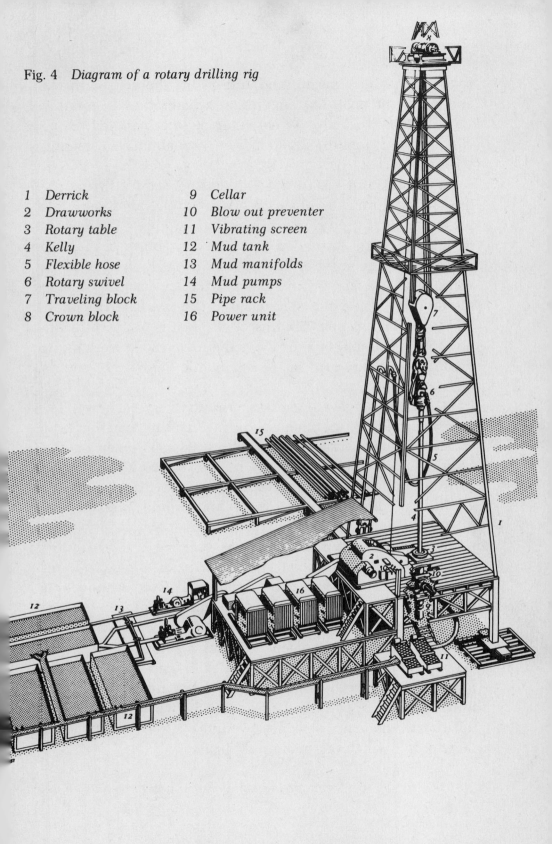

1	Derrick	
2	Drawworks	
3	Rotary table	
4	Kelly	
5	Flexible hose	
6	Rotary swivel	
7	Traveling block	
8	Crown block	

9	Cellar	
10	Blow out preventer	
11	Vibrating screen	
12	Mud tank	
13	Mud manifolds	
14	Mud pumps	
15	Pipe rack	
16	Power unit	

rotate the drill, to pump mud, and to lift the drill string in and out of the hole. The engines are usually diesels, totaling up to 3,700 kw, and may be either directly coupled to the equipment or used to provide power through electric generators and motors.

About one third of the rig power is needed for lifting the drill string. From time to time bits wear out; they may last for hundreds of metres in soft rock, but for only a few metres if a really hard formation is met. To replace a bit, the complete string must be lifted; it is usually unscrewed in sections of 30 metres (three pipes) which are stacked inside the derrick. A new bit is attached to the lowest drill collar, and the string reassembled in sections as it is replaced in the hole. Huge clamps are kept above the rotary table, which can hold the weight of pipe in the hole while the next section is taken on or off.

The hoisting gear must be controlled very accurately so that the pressure on the bit during drilling can be kept constant. If the whole weight of the string is taken on the hoisting gear, the bit will not cut into the rock, but if the entire weight of many hundred metres of steel pipe rested on the bit, it could not be turned and would probably be damaged.

The upper end of the kelly is screwed into a 'rotary swivel' which acts as a stationary bearing on which to hang the drilling string. It also provides a fixed connection through which the drilling mud is pumped into the string. The kelly will drop 10 metres after each section of drill pipe is added and the hole is deepened by this amount, so the line carrying the mud to the swivel must be in the form of flexible hose. The rotary swivel hangs from a very heavy block-and-pulley system, the weight being taken by wire rope of up to 38 mm in diameter, which is wound on to the drum of a large power winch on the derrick floor.

5 *Drilling rig of an exloration well in the Libyan desert*

The derrick itself is a steel tower, usually 41 metres high, standing on a 10-metre square base, about 7 metres above ground level. It looks rather like the pylon for a high-voltage electricity supply, but without the side-arms to hold the cables.

The mud circulation system requires over half the total power of the rig, as it may be necessary to pump over 60 litres per second of fluid mud at pressures up to 240 bar. The mud itself is made up of water with special clays and other minerals. Its composition can be varied from time to time according to the type of rock being drilled.

Mud control is a special science all of its own. The mud must have certain characteristics if it is to be of any use: it must have sufficient body to lift the rock chippings to the surface and prevent them settling to the bottom of the hole when drilling stops; it must lubricate the bit and not abrade it; it must be heavy enough to maintain the desired pressure in the hole; it must give up water under pressure only to the extent necessary to leave a thin layer of near-solid mud on the exposed rock forming the side of the hole. A great deal of research continues into the making of suitable muds for all conditions. This valuable material must not be lost when it returns to the surface, but must be collected for pumping round continuously.

During the course of drilling it is most likely that some rocks will be penetrated which are soft and tend to cave in. Others may contain water, or be porous and tend to absorb the drilling mud. Up to a point these problems can be dealt with while drilling is under way and there is mud pressure in the hole. But sooner or later, something must be done, especially if the hole finds oil and is to be kept open permanently. At intervals, the hole is lined with steel pipe or casing, which is held in place by pumping cement in between the casing and the side of the hole. Naturally, when casing has been put in place, further drilling must be done with a smaller bit which can pass down inside, and the diameter of the hole reduces stepwise as it gets deeper.

A typical programme for bit size and casing might be: for the first 60 metres, use a 585-mm bit and then run casing of about 475 mm in diameter; for the next 1,000 metres, a 445-mm bit and 343-mm casing right to the surface, fixing it in place with cement in the space outside. This continues until the desired total depth is reached, and in a very deep hole the final casing could be as small as 57 mm. The top end of each run of casing is connected into a well head which consists of heavy flanged pipe with a valve system known as a blow-out preventer for controlling high pressures if gas or oil-bearing rock is struck.

As drilling proceeds, it is important to do a number of things to keep the drillers informed of what is going on at the bottom of that narrow hole thousands of metres beneath them. Tests are made from time to time to ensure that the hole is going down straight (or at a constant angle if it has been decided to drill deliberately in this way). The mud engineer and geologist will be examining the mud all the time to find out what sort of rock is being bored, and may be able to find microscopic fossils or fragments of larger ones which will permit an estimate of the geological age of the strata.

The geologist may ask for a 'core sample' to be taken. This involves replacing the bit with a special annular cutter which will cut out a solid cylinder of rock for examination at the surface. Since this operation means taking the entire string out of the hole and running it back twice, once with the core cutter, and again with the bit to resume normal drilling, it is time-consuming. The drilling engineer in charge will not want to do this more often than is absolutely necessary, since drilling is a most expensive operation.

Drilling is also a very skilled job, and a mistake over drill pressure or mud composition can result in losing a bit or breaking off the string or drill pipe. If this happens, special tools are available with which to 'fish' for the lost piece, so that the work does not have to be started all over again at the beginning.

When the bit reaches oil-bearing rock, the first indication may be a rapid rise in the bottom pressure and perhaps the appearance of traces of gas or oil in the returning mud. The blow-out preventer will then function to stop the mud and the drill string from being pushed violently out of the hole, and the mud composition is changed at once to allow for the extra pressure. If the 'show' of oil appears to be substantial, it is allowed to flow to the surface under control. Steps can then be taken to find out how much oil is reaching the bottom of the hole through the surrounding porous rock, and to determine its quality.

If the indications are good, further wells will be drilled in the area to establish the extent of the oil-bearing rocks and the overall size of the oilfield. These wells will be easier to drill, because the drillers will have a good idea of the rock problems they are going to meet on the way down, the extent of difficult rocks and water-bearing zones, and the depth at which oil is likely to be found. While these first production wells are being drilled, a careful assessment must be made of the likely rate of production of crude oil from the field as a whole. Pipes must be laid from individual wells to collect the oil at gathering centres, and equipment designed and erected to separate surplus gas from the oil. A large pipeline and pumps will also be needed, to move the oil to the nearest refinery or port from which it can be shipped.

Many wells contain oil at sufficiently high pressure for it to come to the surface by itself. Others require pumps to bring the oil up. Pumping wells can be seen in many parts of

7 *Pipelaying in Alaska*
   The pipe, already welded, is lowered into a ditch

the United States and in the English Midlands, among other places. Most wells in the Middle East are of the high pressure type which require no pumps.

Deep wells are not the only possible large-scale source of crude oil. Since the middle of the nineteenth century, oil shale has been mined in Scotland, and this industry has only recently ceased to be economic. The shale looks rather like coal, and usable varieties contain 15 percent or more of raw hydrocarbon material which can be recovered by heating, using equipment very like the retorts in a coal-gas works. The further treatment of the oil is simply a variation on the processes used for crude oil.

Oil shale is not very common. The cost of mining and extraction is high compared to conventional crude oil, and left-over rock is hard to dispose of. The huge deposits in Colorado could however be used at some future date. In western Canada, there are huge deposits of another oil-bearing mineral, the Athabasca Tar Sands. The sand contains a large proportion of a heavy crude oil-like material, which can be recovered and treated to make a liquid more like conventional crude. These deposits are now being exploited, but the cost is fairly high because first of all the sand has to be collected by open-cast mining, then it must be separated from the liquid, and finally there is an expensive preparation stage before it can be handled like normal crude oil. The biggest difficulty technically is the separation of solids from the 'tar'; this is now being overcome, so we may see more use made of this valuable alternative to crude oil from wells.

When something goes seriously wrong with a drilling operation, expert help is needed quickly. At one time it was not uncommon for high pressure wells to declare the presence of oil by blowing it out through the derrick and its machinery. This is now rare owing to the improvements in drilling technique and well head equipment. But it still happens occasionally, and a very large fire may result.

There are a few firms who have experts prepared to go at an hour's notice to any part of the world to deal with such disasters. They are a brave and highly skilled band. Some years ago, in South Iran, a new well was being drilled on an established field. It was known that oil and gas would be found at high pressure, and the depth of the oil-bearing layers was accurately predicted.

Just at the most critical time, when the crew was drilling through the cap-rock into the high-pressure strata, the drill-pipe broke, leaving the bit and several thousand feet of pipe down the hole. The first job was to get special tools into the hole to fish out the broken pipe. Because of the high pressure below, things went wrong when the pipe was picked up, and the well blew out, destroying the derrick and damaging much of the other surface equipment. Gas rushed out and ignited, turning the whole area into a raging inferno of flame and noise, covered with a pall of smoke going thousands of feet up into the air.

The safest thing for the moment was to let the fire burn. The greatest oil fire expert of the day was Myron Kinley and he was sent for from California. In three days he was at the well, ready to inspect the fire and decide how to control it. First, he had a temporary road bulldozed into the area; then he had water piped up from the nearest river and part of the valley in which the well was located was turned into a small reservoir. The next job was to inspect the fire closely. Kinley had a screen built of corrugated iron and asbestos sheeting, and this was pushed forward by a bulldozer under a deluge of water from fire-hoses.

The tangled wreckage, which had been spreading flames in all directions from the well head, was cleared with a large explosive charge. When the well head was blown off, the pressure lifted half a mile of 114 mm pipe out of the hole, just like a gigantic string of spaghetti. Then, after drenching the area with water for a week to cool things down, the single remaining flame, 300 metres high, was blown out like a candle with a second explosive charge.

The fire was extinguished, but gas was blowing from the hole as violently as ever. So the final stage was the most dangerous of all, because the smallest spark would have produced an explosion wiping out all the men and equipment in the area. Under these conditions, the top of the well casing was prepared for fitting a new valve. A special, very heavy valve was brought in, and lowered over the gas jet with infinite care, bolted in place and slowly closed. The month long, ear-splitting scream of escaping gas died to a roar, then to a whisper, and finally to total silence. A well (and prehaps the production of a whole oilfield) was saved by the ingenuity and daring of one man, supported by a skillful and courageous team.

We shall see later on how the supplies are moved, and also how various refining processes are used to turn the oil into more valuable and readily used products.

5 · The Nature of Oil

Crude petroleum is only of limited use to us in the form in which it is found, unless we happen upon one of its more extreme forms, such as natural gas or pure bitumen. It is possible to burn more or less any crude oil in an industrial-size boiler or furnace, but this would be very wasteful since it is possible to obtain from crude oil a wide variety of products and still have an industrial fuel as a residue.

People are most aware of the oil products such as gasoline, oil and grease, and lamp kerosene, which are in daily use by individuals. They are also aware that diesel fuel, gas for camping stoves, aircraft fuels and industrial fuel oils are all products of the petroleum industry, along with a mysterious thing called petro-chemical feedstock and a variety of other oils which are used in relatively small quantities, mainly by other industries. Knowledge of how all these things are related, and how they are made from crude oil, is not so widespread.

Crude oil is an extremely complex mixture, consisting of

thousands of different chemical substances. Only a few hundred of these have been identified exactly despite many years of work in laboratories all over the world, and the oil chemists are still busy on this job. We do know, however, a great deal about the simpler substances which turn up in crude oil, about the main classes of substance present, and about the proportions in which each appears in specific kinds of crude. All these substances have one thing in common— they are compounds containing hydrogen and carbon. The bulk of any oil consists of substances containing these two elements alone, but there are also small amounts of compounds with other elements, notably sulphur, oxygen, nitrogen, and traces of a number of metals. Clearly we are mainly concerned with those compounds of hydrogen and carbon only—the hydrocarbons. The substances containing other elements are generally regarded as impurities, but their chemistry can be important because it is often desirable and sometimes absolutely necessary to get rid of them in the course of manufacturing finished oil products.

Because crude oil is a mixture of many substances, it has no fixed boiling point, but appears to boil away steadily as the temperature is increased. Individual components have boiling points from $-161°$ to around $1000°C$. The mixture is a dark liquid, usually with quite a strong smell. Most crude oils are not very viscous; that is, they are fairly 'thin' liquids which flow easily. For those readers who have studied a little chemistry, more about the types of compound which occur in petroleum is given in an appendix at the end of the book.

Crude oils from different parts of the world, or even from different parts of the same oilfield are never quite the same, though the quality from a particular well or from a producing area taken as a whole is often remarkably constant over a period of years. The differences arise because the proportions of various hydrocarbons in the oil are different. Some crude

oils have a lot of high-boiling material in them, others may
have very little. Some contain a lot of the compounds made
up from rings of carbon atoms, others have mainly chain-
type compounds. (See appendix). We make use of the
different types of crude oil according to the kind of products
we want to make, and the quantities of different products
which are required at any particular time and place.

Chemically, the hydrocarbons which occur in crude oil
are compounds which do not react very easily with each
other or with other chemicals. There are of course degrees of
reactivity and in refining we can make use of the fact that
some classes of compound can be made to enter into
chemical reactions more easily than others. There are a
number of ways of altering the chemical make-up of various
parts of crude oil, and so varying the quantity and type of
products made. We can select which sort of alteration
process we use, to suit the products wanted and the kind of
crude oil available.

Fortunately, from the point of view of the refiner, the
things in crude oil which we are likely to want to get rid of,
such as sulphur compounds, are more reactive with a range
of chemicals than are the hydrocarbons. The unwanted
materials can either be removed completely, or are sometimes converted into forms in which they will be harmless in
the end use of the product. For instance, the commonest type
of sulphur compound, particularly in the lower-boiling part
of crude oil, is the mercaptan.

There are three ways in common use of getting rid of
mercaptans, which are smelly and have other objectionable
properties. The first method is to dissolve the mercaptan in a
mixture of caustic soda solution with other chemicals. A
second way is to convert the mercaptan into another and less
objectionable type of sulphur compound with the aid of
copper chloride. The copper chloride is used as a catalyst,

that is, a material which assists by speeding up a reaction without itself being altered in the process. The third method of removing mercaptan is also catalytic, and this one will remove all other kinds of sulphur compound. Hydrogen is used at high temperature and pressure, and the sulphur compounds are converted to the basic hydrocarbon plus hydrogen sulphide. The hydrogen sulphide must then be got rid of separately.

If, therefore, the best use is to be made of the crude oils found in the ground, it is most important to know as much as possible about the composition of the oil before trying to process it in a refinery. As soon as a new well has been proved to contain useful quantities of oil, the men who have drilled the well take samples of the oil and send it to the research laboratories which are run by all large oil companies or to an independent laboratory for analysis.

The chemists in these laboratories find out how much of the oil boils in successive temperature ranges, determine as far as possible which individual hydrocarbon compounds are present, and how much sulphur and other impurities may have to be dealt with. They collect the various boiling ranges or 'cuts' by distilling the crude oil. The cuts are examined separately to see what use can best be made of them in the manufacture of finished products, and what refining treatments may be needed.

This type of work is going on all the time, since exploration and the discovery of new sources of crude oil is a continuous job. Oil companies obviously need to know all about the crude oils which they have found for themselves. They also need to examine samples from other companies, since they may wish to buy supplies from others to add to the types and quantities available in order to make a full range of products. A lot of this work becomes a regular routine, using the same tests again and again on samples from different places, since it is necessary to compare the different crude oils under standard conditions. At the same time, however, a great deal of effort is devoted to looking for quicker methods of analysis and ways of getting more information about the detailed composition of the oil.

Research workers in chemistry and physics are always in demand to work out new methods of analysis, and to apply these methods in furthering our understanding of the nature of crude oil. The results are passed on to other workers in refineries and in the research laboratories, who can use them to improve old processes and invent new ones for making more and better products out of the crude oil which is the basic raw material of the industry.

6 · The Right Oil for the Right Purpose

By far the greater part of the product of the oil industry is fuel which will be burnt in one way or another to provide heat energy, either as an open flame or in a motor. Only the lubricating oils and greases, the wax, bitumen and solvents, remain in use in the form in which they leave the refinery and are not destroyed instantly when put to use. The petrochemical feedstocks are manufactured by oil refiners only to be taken to another type of factory and converted into something entirely different. They are mainly used to produce the chemical parts for making plastics, synthetic fibres and synthetic rubber, and solvents for a wide variety of industrial uses.

Nearly all crude oils contain some light, low-boiling hydrocarbons which are gases at normal temperatures—methane, ethane, propane and butane. These gases also appear as byproducts from some of the more complex refinery processes. That is, they are not made intentionally, but come into being in relatively small quantities. This takes place as a result of the chemical breakdown of part of the feedstock, in a process intended primarily to make something quite different.

The propane and butane, or mixtures of these two gases, can be liquefied under moderate pressures of up to about 7 bar at normal temperatures. In this form they can be moved in specially constructed road-cars to large industrial users, or they can be put into strong metal bottles to be sold for domestic use in camping stoves or for light and heat in districts where there is no other source of domestic power. They are quite easily separated from the rest of the crude oil, but usually contain foul-smelling sulphur compounds which must be removed. For use in houses, something else has to be put back with a strong but less unpleasant smell so that leaks can be detected in the same way as with coal gas. Gas which cannot be sold is sometimes used to make other products in the refinery, and any that is left over is used for fuel.

The most publicised product is undoubtedly gasoline for automobiles. It is a very important product in any country, and in the United States and Canada it accounts for nearly half the total output of the industry. It boils between 0° and 200°C, and in the early days of the industry it was very easy to make—they just took the appropriate part of the crude oil, treated it a little chemically so that it would not smell too horrible, and sold it to the motorist. That has all changed, except that we still use oil of the same boiling range. The modern motorist has come to expect a great deal of his fuel. The engine of his car must not knock or 'ping' under any conditions; it must start easily on cold mornings and must not stall in a traffic jam on a hot summer day; it must give good mileage to the gallon, and of course it must not be too expensive. Rightly, he expects the oil company selling the gasoline to have thought about all these things.

The most important things in making a good gasoline are

to balance the different materials which go into it so that the engine will receive a satisfactory mixture through the carburetor whatever the temperature of the machinery and its surroundings, and to ensure that the knock-rating or octane number is suitable for the particular engine. To achieve the first of these objects a limit is set to the temperature at which a given amount of the petrol will boil off. The tests used to control volatility vary, but they all have the same aim, and the volatility, or tendency to boil, is adjusted to suit the climate in which the petrol will be used. Knock-rating is measured by a special test engine which runs under standard conditions of speed, temperature and air mixture on a stationary test bed, and the test fuel is compared with mixtures of standard fuels of known knock-rating.

8   *CFR test engine for measuring the knock-rating of motor fuels*

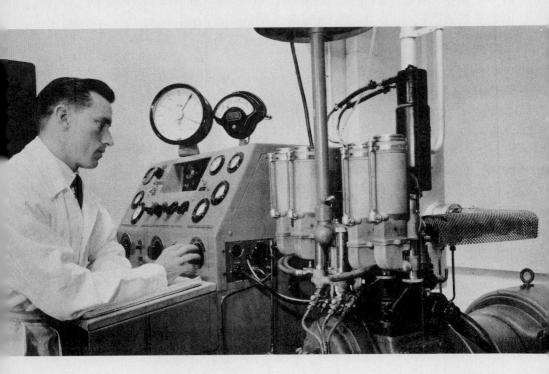

The result of the test is expressed as an octane number, and premium motor spirit in most countries has an octane number in the range of 97–99. The octane number for regular and non-leaded grades is commonly 90–94. Small amounts of additives are put in to improve certain properties. Tetra-ethyl lead has been widely used, but it is now being reduced or eliminated to meet clean air requirements.

A continual check is kept of the requirements of new models produced by the motor industry. This side of the work may involve special tests in desert or arctic conditions, plus the most careful examination by the oil companies' research organizations of any reactions from customers. The same sort of investigation is needed if a company wishes to start selling gasoline made by new processes or containing new additives. In addition to laboratory and test-track work at home, it may be necessary to send vehicles, along with the new fuels and scientists to observe their behaviour, to places with the most extreme hot or cold climates.

All older types and modern light aircraft use piston engines working on the same principles as those in cars. The fuel used in piston-engined aircraft is therefore a special development of motor gasoline, made to take care of the light high-powered engines which are needed for flight. The larger engines require fuel with a very high knock-rating, and all need special volatility controls.

Since the middle 1950's, the jet engine has taken over for most aircraft used in long-distance international flights and on domestic routes, with the result that the major airlines need very little other than jet fuel. When the first jets or aircraft turbine engines were built, it was hoped that they would burn almost anything. It is still true that turbine engines used for ground jobs, such as driving electrical generators, can burn a wide variety of fuels from gas to residual fuel oil. Aircraft, however, are a great deal more critical, for reasons connected with the way in which they are used rather than with the nature of the engine itself.

The most important factors in choosing the type of fuel to use in aircraft and the way of making it are concerned with flight safety. If your car engine stopped suddenly, it would be inconvenient and it could possibly be dangerous. If an aircraft suddenly loses power altogether, it is almost certain that the machine will be wrecked and highly likely that people will be killed. To be sure the fuel is reliable, a number of conditions must be met. The fuel must be free of solid particles which could block filters or damage delicate engine parts. It must be virtually free of water, since this might separate out (even forming ice in the cold conditions at high altitude) and stop the engine. It must be quite incapable of corroding any part of the finely-engineered fuel pumps. It must not go solid when very cold, or the pumps will refuse to move it from the tanks to the engines.

In addition, the airline or air force buying the fuel wants good value for money in terms of the amount of power which can be developed from a given weight of fuel. Because the air pressure at great heights is very low, liquids boil more easily, and it is not possible to use a very low-boiling fuel as it could evaporate away during flight. Most users also want a fairly high-boiling fuel since this will catch fire less easily if there should be an accident. The fuel must of course burn cleanly in the engine, or it will make an excessive amount of smoke and will not give all the power it should.

All these considerations, and a few others besides, have led to the use of only two main types of fuel for aircraft turbine engines. One is kerosene, boiling between about 150° and 250°C, which is used by most commercial airlines. A special variant of this fuel is used for operations from aircraft carriers, and for safety reasons this is a selected material of the lowest possible inflammability. The other main type is a so-called 'wide-cut' fuel, boiling between about 30° and 240°C. This is used largely by military aircraft, because it is a bit cheaper and in wartime could be made more easily, in very large quantities.

Not only must manufacture of these fuels be most carefully controlled, but the greatest care is taken in handling them at every step on their way to the aircraft, so that nothing harmful can get into them. The final stage is in the fueling trucks seen at an airport. These contain filters capable of throwing out all but a few parts per million of water and removing any dirt larger than five-thousandths of a millimetre across.

Some possible changes and improvements in aircraft fuels have been proposed in recent years. Two lines of development are concerned with improving safety. The first proposal is to provide fuel in the form of an emulsion of oil in a very small quantity of water (about 3 percent), using special chemicals to prevent the emulsion separating into two layers of oil and water. This emulsion can be burned without difficulty in the controlled conditions inside an engine, but could greatly reduce the hazards in accidental fires. The second idea is to use chemicals which will turn the fuel instantly into a jelly, injecting the chemical only if a crash seems imminent. The object in this case is to get the fuel into a form in which it cannot easily splash around if the tanks split open. This reduces the risk of fire. Another line of investigation is towards using liquefied gas as aircraft fuel, the object being to provide a cheaper fuel, and one which would help out if the more usual kinds were to run short. The gas would be chilled to very low temperatures so that it could be loaded on the aircraft as a liquid.

Each of these proposals could be brought to the point of everyday use within the next few years, though each bristles with problems. The possibilities here serve to demonstrate a

9 *A large jet is refueled at John F. Kennedy International
Airport, New York City*

chain of events which must be followed in every technical
advance made by man, not only in the oil industry. First,
someone must have an idea, the first stage of invention. Then
the idea must be shown to be technically possible, having in
mind the knowledge avilable in other skills and sciences
which may be needed to perfect it. Thirdly, the mechanism
must be made practical, that is, safe and reasonably convenient to use for people who may not know all the scientific
principles behind it. Finally, the whole thing must be
commercially sound. Every time industry introduces a new
or improved product to the public these steps must be gone
through, and the final test is always the same—can you put it
on the market at a price the customers are willing to pay?

Petroleum fuels for rockets are generally of the kerosene type. They are similar to the kerosene used for jet aircraft, but the fuel may have to be somewhat more highly refined to obtain properties which would not normally be of importance for use comparatively near the ground. As with aircraft, it is vitally important that nothing should go wrong due to impurities or other shortcomings of the fuel, and the properties required are laid down very exactly.

Another light distillate product which is wanted nowadays in huge quantities is the feedstock used in petrochemical factories. A considerable proportion of the light gasoline boiling between 30° and 150°C goes into this type of product.

Although the demand for petrochemical feedstock is large, it does not by any means absorb all the available petroleum distillate boiling below 150°C. Some is used in widecut aviation turbine fuel, and much is used either directly or after special processing in motor gasolines. There is also a small but important group of petroleum solvents within this boiling range and extending up to about 200°C. They are used to dissolve other materials for chemical processes and as the 'carrier solvents' for paints, adhesives, liquid polishes, printing inks and the like.

The most familiar of these solvents is probably white spirit or turpentine substitute, an essential ingredient of most oil-based paints. White spirit is one of the heavier petroleum solvents, boiling between 150°C and 200°C, and is chosen so that it will not be too inflammable for safe household use. Also among these 'special boiling point solvents' are the fuels used in cigarette lighters, and special solvents for extracting the vegetable oils used in making things like soap and margarine.

All these solvents boil over fairly narrow ranges, usually not more than 50°C, and must be specially prepared from

10 *The tanks of a DC-8 are connected to a BP fuelling truck*

crude oil. They need to be highly purified so as to have little
or no odour and no harmful effects upon those who use them
or the other products with which they will come in contact.
The most important factor in this purification is the removal
of all except the smallest traces of sulphur compounds and
potentially poisonous substances like benzene.

The kerosene fraction from crude oil used for aviation
turbine fuel also forms an important part of domestic
furnace oil, especially that used in colder parts of the country
in winter. This winter, or arctic, grade is virtually the same
as aviation kerosene, except that it does not need to go
through the special cleaning-up stages. The property that is
probably the most critical for domestic heating is that it
should flow freely from storage tanks even in the coldest
weather.

For the older types of kerosene lamp and small room
heaters, a special kind of purified kerosene is still needed in
small quantities. This is premium kerosene or paraffin. The
most important feature of paraffins in the kerosene boiling
range is that they burn with a clear almost smokeless flame.
Premium kerosene is made by extracting the smoky-burning
hydrocarbons and most of the sulphur and using the extracted material for other purposes.

A final product belonging to the kerosene group is tractor
vaporising oil, at one time widely used for tractors, but now
very largely displaced by diesel fuels. TVO is for practical
purposes a very low grade petrol, with a much higher boiling
range than that used for modern cars.

Many years ago, it was found that a substitute for coal-gas
could be made from certain petroleum fractions or cuts of
specified boiling range, and a heavy distillate oil which at
that time had little other use was widely favoured. This oil
was mostly used in gas works to run small convertors which
could be started up quickly to help out at times of peak load,

and it came to be known as gas oil. Nowadays, coal-gas has been replaced by natural gas wherever this fuel is available, or else gas is made by the conversion of refinery waste gas, of light distillates similar to petrochemical feedstocks, and of residual fuel oils. The name 'gas oil' has stuck to distillate fuels boiling in the range around 200° to 350°C, although nearly all of this oil is used for very different purposes. The main uses are now for small and medium-sized heating installations and for all diesel engines except the largest marine types.

The requirements for a heating oil are quite simple. The burners are designed by the boiler manufacturer to handle the range of viscosities likely to be met with in commercial gas oils and at the same time give clean and complete combustion. The oil must not solidify at the lowest winter temperatures likely to be reached in outdoor tanks. This property can be controlled by altering the distillation range of the fuel, since the higher-boiling materials tend to solidify at higher temperatures. For very cold places, such as Canada and the mid-Continent, it is necessary to use an oil entirely boiling in the kerosene range. Manufacture is controlled by observing the pour point, or temperature at which the oil refuses to flow freely. In addition, many governments and local authorities, who are interested in keeping the air clean and pure, set limits on the sulphur content of fuels which may be burnt in their areas. This can be looked after by choosing gas oil from a crude oil which has a low natural sulphur content, or by special processing in the refinery to remove sulphur. In the United States and Europe most normal domestic fuels are of this type.

Gas oils used for diesel engines are rather more specialised. Large, medium- or low-speed diesels are usually quite content with the same quality as that which is sold as heating oil, but the high-speed diesel engines used in trucks and buses are more difficult to suit. Firstly, because the exhaust fumes will be emitted at street level, it becomes important to avoid air pollution by limiting sulphur content. Sulphur is also corrosive to engine parts, especially under the severe conditions which may arise in a high-speed engine. Low temperature properties are also more vital. For one thing it is not possible to protect the fuel tank in any way against the cold. Then there is a tendency for wax crystals to form well above the pour point, and these can block fuel filters on the way to the engine. The filters cannot safely be left off, so we must ensure that the wax is not likely to form at the lowest temperature which the fuel is likely to meet in service. This can be done by observing the cloud point, which is the temperature at which wax visibly begins to separate.

Finally, there are the burning properties in the engine to be considered. One can test the fuel in a stationary engine in the same sort of way that is used for rating motor spirits, and produce a cetane number rating. But this is rarely done, as the test method is tedious, and there is an alternative method for assessing engine performance. An index number can be calculated from other fuel properties, such as specific gravity and distillation characteristics, which corresponds closely to the engine test cetane number and is much quicker to obtain. As for any internal combustion engine fuel, the diesel oil must not give rise to deposits of carbon and gum in the engine, and it must be reasonably free from dirt and water.

In terms of world-wide consumption, one of the most important groups of products is the rather unglamorous black residual fuel oil. This fuel is made from what is left of the crude oil after all the other products have been taken out. The residual fuels are the staple of industry, and are used to fire the big boilers in factories and power stations, in many types of industrial furnace, for steam raising in big ships, and in steel and glass works.

The burners used for residual fuel are mostly of the atomising type, in other words the flow of liquid fuel is broken up into fine droplets which will burn cleanly and easily as they pass out from the burner nozzle. The simplest of these burners relies on a supply of oil at fairly high pressure, flowing into a specially constructed burner tip which breaks up the flow by swirling it round in a small chamber just before the final nozzle. Others use air or steam, or mechanically rotated parts to break up the oil flow. In every case, the burner will work properly only if the oil is fed to it at the correct viscosity or thickness. It is possible to choose the viscosity of the fuel by selecting the crude oil from which it is made, and by regulating the amount of lighter oil which is blended with the residue. All liquids become more fluid (less viscous) as temperature increases, so the viscosity of the oil reaching the burner can be further regulated by controlling the temperature at which it is supplied.

As with the lighter heating oils, it is important that the oil should flow freely from the storage tanks to the preheater and pumps. The pour point, therefore, must not be too high. This is not very critical in big industrial installations, since it can usually be arranged for the storage tanks to be fitted with steam coils to heat the oil above its pour point at all times. Not all customers, however, want to have the trouble and expense of tank heating. It may also be necessary to deliver the oil in unheated road or rail tank cars in cold weather, so pour point can still be an important factor with residual fuel oils, especially in cold climates.

Many countries limit by law the maximum amount of sulphur in fuel oils which will be burnt within their boundaries; in addition, the height of chimneys is frequently regulated according to the amount of oxides of sulphur which may be discharged from them during the course of a day. The latter sort of rule normally applies only to factories.

In glass and steel making and some other manufacturing processes where the hot gases from oil burning can come in direct contact with the product, a very low sulphur content fuel may be needed. So, one way and another, there is an increasing demand for fuel oils with low sulphur content. This is not easy to meet, since many of the most readily available crude oils contain substantial amounts of sulphur, largely concentrated in the residue. Kuwait and Arabian crude oils, for example, are available in huge amounts and are the cheapest of imported crudes. Unfortunately their residue sulphur contents around 4 percent are far too high for clean air laws in many areas. To make use of them, therefore, the oil must be desulphurised or else the flue gas must be cleaned of sulphur oxides before it leaves the chimney. Means are available for either route to reducing sulphur emissions, but all are expensive to install and operate, and have so far seen use only in limited areas with special problems.

It may seem a little odd that we should have to worry about ash in a liquid fuel, though we take it for granted when we are burning coal or wood. Ash may, nevertheless, be a serious problem. There are minute amounts of metallic compounds in the residues from most crude oils, amounting perhaps to 100 parts in every million in a typical crude. Some of the metals are chemically part of the crude oil, others come up with the small amounts of mineral bearing water which is found in many oil wells. There is not much trouble with fine ash coming out of chimneys, but some of the metals present in the oil can lay down deposits on boiler tubes. These deposits reduce the efficiency of the boiler over a period of time, and may also corrode the metal from which the tubes are made. Some types of boiler suffer more than others, and care must be taken not to give high metal content oil to the more critical installations.

The black fuel oils are made mainly from crude oil residues boiling above about 350°C, and most of the residue finds its way into this kind of product. However, certain special products can be made after further separation of the residue by distillation. These special products are needed only in relatively small quantities, and are not made in all oil refineries. A very heavy residue, boiling above about 550°C from a suitable crude oil, is bitumen, the main use for which is in road making. For this job, bitumen from crude oil has largely replaced coal tars and the natural bitumen found in places like the Trinidad Pitch Lake. The important feature of bitumen is that it should remain more or less solid so that the road surface will not melt in hot weather, but at the same time it must be sufficiently flexible for the surface not to crack under heavy loads.

But what can be done with the part of the oil boiling between 350° and 550°C? We can of course return it to fuel oil, and there are some other uses to which it can be put in the refinery, but it is also the starting material for making most lubricating oils. From the refiner's point of view, the most important properties which must be achieved in a lubricating oil are three. Firstly, it must not go solid at the temperature likely to be reached when the engine is shut down, or it may not be possible to start it again. Secondly, it must not become too thin at the operating temperature of the engine, or lubrication may fail and the engine freeze up. Thirdly, it must be able to resist the tendency to burn when subjected to high temperatures in the engine for prolonged periods.

All these things can be looked after by choosing suitable crude oils and putting the appropriate distillate through certain additional processes. Sometimes it is also necessary to add other chemicals to the finished lubricant to reach the standards needed in modern high-speed machinery.

7 · Oil Products

The plastics industry is a perfect example of how research and development work leads to production on an enormous scale, given a few good ideas and a demand for new and better products. A large part of plastics manufacture, and a great deal of other chemical industry, depends directly on oil for its raw material. Indeed, a number of oil companies now do the whole job themselves very profitably, because the manufacture of petrochemicals, including plastics, gives them a certain regular outlet for part of the production from their refineries.

From the chemist's point of view, the link between the oil industry and these other diverse products is a straightforward one. Petrochemicals are built up from the same chemical elements found in oil, sometimes with other things added. Accordingly, selected oil refinery products can be used to make the basic raw materials from which the other new materials can be built. Two of the commonest basic building materials in the industrial organic chemist's stock are the gases ethylene and propylene.

These substances are hardly to be found at all in crude oil, and are only produced in fairly small amounts among the by-products of normal refining processes. They can, however, be made in large amounts by heating light petroleum distillates strongly under pressure in the presence of steam. The distillate used is gasoline boiling between about 30° and 150°C. The 'aromatic' liquids, benzene, toluene and xylene can also be made in large quantities by processes which are now a normal part of the oil refiner's stock-in-trade. These too have extensive use in petrochemical manufacture.

The uses of petrochemicals, and the ways in which they are made from a few basic types of raw material, would make a whole book in themselves. A list of the main types of petrochemical product will help to show the diversity and importance of these comparative newcomers to industry.

Petrochemicals may turn up as all or part of any of the following things: synthetic fibres for clothing, notably nylon, Terylene, rayon; synthetic rubber for tyres and many other uses; carbon black, which is also used in tyre manufacture; plastics, particular examples being Polythene, polystyrene, PVC and a number of synthetic resins. They also take the form of explosives, dyestuffs, fertilisers, detergents, solvents for all sorts of industrial uses; alcohols for industrial use, anti-freeze for cars, insecticides, solvents and emulsions for lacquers and paints; anti-knock fluid used in motor spirit; and finally, refrigerants, adhesives and fire extinguisher fluids.

The petrochemical industry has grown from nothing in the past fifty years. Most of its present major products have been brought into wide use in the home or the factory within the past twenty-five years. This is really a very short time, but long enough for it to be quite hard for anyone born within that time to imagine a world without things like Polythene, nylon, liquid detergents, and many other things which depend on petroleum for their manufacture.

There are other things, too, some old, some new, which are important by-products of the oil industry. In order to get the low temperature properties needed in lubricating oils, it is necessary among other things to remove wax, so here we have yet another useful by-product. Waxes are used for making candles, waxed papers for food-wrapping, water-proofing, electrical insulation and polishes. Closely related to these waxes are the petroleum jellies, which are used in very highly refined form for making cosmetics and ointments. 'Vaseline' is the trade name for the petroleum jelly made by one particular company, but it is a name which has come into common use to describe the similar products made by others. In making waxes and jellies, the melting point, hardness and degree of refinement must all be controlled according to the needs of the end product.

Greases are made from a mixture of oil and specially prepared soaps. They are essentially lubricants for applications which require a relatively high melting point so that they will remain in contact with the metal surfaces which they are to protect without the assistance of pump pressure.

One of the most exciting recent developments in the oil industry has been the discovery that foodstuffs can be made from some parts of crude oil. Types of yeast exist which are able to use oil as the main item in their food supply. The yeasts grow and multiply rapidly, and they can be extracted from the oil, separated and dried for use as a protein supplement in animal foodstuffs. We can use gas oil or certain products derived from it as the raw material for the yeasts to work on, and they will make about a ton of protein concentrate for every ton of oil used up. The oil left over is usable for more conventional purposes; indeed it is improved in some respects. We are not yet able to produce oil protein in an attractive enough form for human food, but one company has already announced its plans for full-scale factories to make the animal food.

In running the refining side of the oil business, quantities of products manufactured must be in balance at all times, since market demand in different parts of the world cannot be changed quickly, and there are strict limits to the amounts which can be stored up. The choice of refining processes is dictated by the product balance, as well as by the quality required and the total demand for all kinds of oil.

Consider just two important oil-consuming areas, the United States and Western Europe, and ignore the total quantities of oil used in each. The following table gives the approximate percentages by weight of major groups of oil products which are used in each area:

PRODUCT	USA	W. EUROPE
Motor fuel/Petrochemical feed	43	17
Kerosene	7	5
Gas/Diesel oils	22	27
Residual fuels	6	37
Other	22	14

The differences in demand for various products in the two areas are large, although both are highly industrialized. These differences reflect variations in the economies and the way of life on either side of the Atlantic. One of the features of industrialized countries with a high standard of living is a large number of private cars. This accounts for the high gasoline demand in the United States, and this is accentuated by the fact that diesel engines are used less on heavy vehicles in that country than they are in Europe.

A look at similar figures for less industrialized countries

shows other significant facts. Asia, Africa and South America tend to have a high demand for kerosene for lamps and stoves, and a fairly small part of their demands in the form of fuel oil. Special factors may distort the expected pattern of consumption. For example, the industrial use of fuel oil in Kuwait and Saudi Arabia is quite small, but their crude oil exporting terminals supply large amounts of residual fuel for ships' bunkers.

The fuel oil needs of South Africa are usually quite low, despite the fact that there is plenty of industrial activity, but this can be explained by the availability of a cheap alternative fuel, in this case mainly coal. These considerations, and forecasts of how and where economic development will take place, have a most important bearing on the way that oil companies plan the future expansion of their refining and trading activities.

Until fairly recently, it was generally assumed that, since there is still more oil in the ground than ever came out of it, there was no real possibility of future shortage. Large discoveries in more remote parts of the world, including under the sea, tended to enhance this feeling of security. But more recently, even given the economic development of the tar sand and shale deposits in North America, there has no longer been the same confidence that supply can be kept ahead of rapidly expanding demand.

Regardless of international politics, oil is bound to become more expensive relative to other existing fuels or newly developed energy sources. It is therefore important that no fuel should be used wastefully, or for purposes which can be better fulfilled by some alternative. Oil will continue for many years to be a very major part of the world's energy supply, but the ways in which it is used and the balance of refinery products are very certain to change substantially.

11   *Completed well head, Libya*

8 · Making the Products: the First Stage

No two crude oils from different areas have quite the same composition; they vary in the amounts and qualities of various products which we can extract from them. The final products which reach the market can be partly described in terms of their boiling ranges; for example, petrochemical feedstocks: 30–150°C; kerosene: 150–250°C; gas oil: 200–350°C. Before the final purification and blending can be completed, these fractions or 'cuts' from crude oil have to be sorted out and the first stage is invariably distillation.

The distillation process can be demonstrated very easily in a suitably equipped laboratory with distillation and receiving flasks, a simple fractionating column, a water-cooled condenser and thermometers. A sample of crude oil is needed, and apparatus which is completely safe for handling highly inflammable products.

Let us suppose that the apparatus has been assembled, and the distillation flask is about half full of crude oil. When heat is applied, boiling will start almost at once. The first thing to come off would be gas. This would be lost as the condenser would not be cold enough to recondense it. The temperature at the column head when the first drops of liquid fall into the receiver is noted, and the experiment continued by distilling slowly until the temperature reaches about 150°C. It would be convenient to stop the heating at this point, change receivers and collect the fraction 150–250°C, and similarly the fraction 250–350°C. This is about as far as one could go, because glass apparatus would not stand the strain, and also under these conditions the remaining oil would start to break down or 'crack', with production of rather dense white fumes.

Suppose that there are now four fractions, including the residue in the distillation flask. The first is a gasoline cut, which will be a thin volatile liquid, colourless and rather smelly. Its specific gravity will be the lowest of the four. The second fraction, collected when the column-head temperature was between 150 and 250°C, is kerosene. It would be possible to re-distil this one and check that it does actually boil in approximately this range. This fraction should also be colourless; it would be rather more viscous than the first and probably have a less strong odour. The third fraction is gas oil; it would be appreciably more viscous, and is likely to be yellow or brownish. If made cold enough, it would go solid. The residue in the distillation flask would be black and very viscous—probably it could not be got out of the flask without warming it up again. The amounts collected in each fraction would depend on the source of the crude oil, and also on the precise cut-points between the fractions.

This experiment is the basis of all oil refining, because it is the only practical way in which to set about the large-scale separation of the end products. Clearly, there would be difficulties in scaling up this experiment to handle thousands of tons of oil a day, so, as in most modern industry, we look for a way of arranging a continuous process. The simple laboratory fractionating column works because the top is cooled by the air while the flask at the bottom is being heated. This allows the lowest-boiling vapours which are rising at any moment to pass over to the condenser, while the heavier vapours tend to condense on the sides of the column and run back towards the flask. The constant re-mixing of light vapour with the descending liquid slows down the overall rate at which liquid boils off and passes to the receiver. This allows a more complete separation to be made of liquids whose boiling points lie close together. However, separation only approaches completeness if we can arrange for a very large proportion of the vapour to condense within the column and flow back for re-mixing and re-boiling—this is called a high reflux rate.

In the laboratory experiment, the temperatures throughout the column increase steadily as more and more of the lower-boiling fractions are boiled off and collected at the end of the condenser. This is the major difference between the experiment and a continuous full-scale job. In designing the commercial distillation column, we arrange for temperature conditions to be constant at any point, feed oil in continuously, and draw off the distillates and residue the whole time. The crude oil normally goes in partway up the column, and products at chosen levels can be taken off above this point as well as from the top.

The inside of a refinery distillation column is quite complicated. So is the main equipment outside which enables it all to work. An empty column would not do the job required, since there would be nothing to ensure re-mixing of the uprising oil vapours with the down-flowing liquid. So the column is divided up into sections by horizontal 'trays' with large numbers of holes in them. The vapours pass up through these holes, and are then forced to pass through a shallow

12 *Stack of bubble caps on their trays,
removed from distillation column for overhaul*

layer of liquid on the tray, so that vapour and liquid become well mixed as they pass one another. One simple device for mixing is the 'bubble cap' and there are many others.

There may be from twenty to sixty trays in a distillation column, depending on the purpose for which it is designed, and they are usually 1½—2 feet apart. The diameter of the column will depend on the amount of oil which is to be distilled, and the main column on a crude oil distillation unit might be 10—15 feet across. At the point where we wish to draw off side-cuts or intermediate fractions, special trays are put in, designed so that part of the liquid will flow to one side and pass out to another small column with only a few trays, known as a stripper. The purpose of the stripper is to remove small amounts of vapour from the liquid entering it, which really belong in the next lighter cut up the main column.

To provide extra heat to assist the separation of this vapour, a small amount of steam is passed into the base of

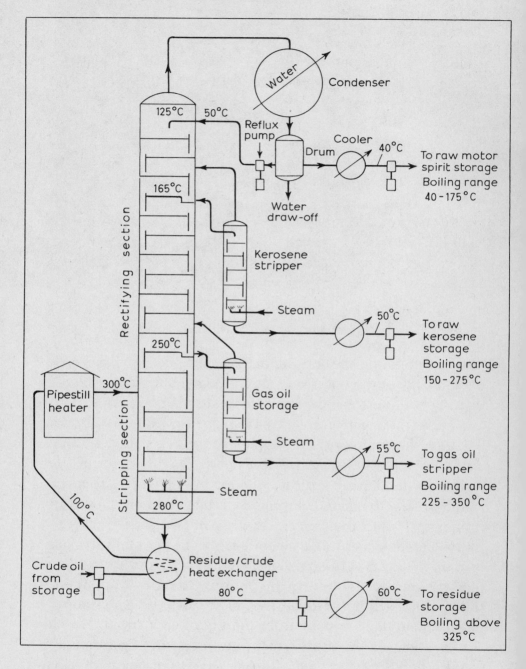

Fig. 5 *Diagram of a distillation column*

the stripper. The vapour passes back to the main column through a separate pipe from the top of the stripper. It is also usual to inject open steam at low pressure into the base of the main column to assist separation of the residue from the gas oil which is the lowest side-cut.

The crude oil must be heated before it gets to the column, and the heater used is known as a 'pipestill'. This is an oil- or gas-fired furnace which may be the size of quite a large house. The oil or gas burners project inwards through the walls near ground level. The oil to be heated is pumped through rows of pipes which are mounted on the inside walls. In a crude distillation unit pipestill the oil may be heated to over 300°C, and the temperature of the hot flue gases may be over 800°C.

As the fractions from the crude oil come out of the distillation column, vapors from the column top pass through wide pipes to a condenser, cooled by water or air. This serves the same purpose as the laboratory condenser, but like nearly everything else in the unit, it is made of steel, and is of suitably large size. The condensed vapors are led away into a large receiver, which is a steel tank of several thousand gallons capacity. From the receiver, part of the condensed light oil is pumped away to a storage tank, but a large part of it is returned as reflux to keep the top of the column cooled to the desired constant temperature. Since the residue from the bottom of the column is very hot, it must be cooled before it can be sent to a storage tank. This heat can be used to warm up the crude oil charge before it enters the pipestill, and so save on the cost of pipestill fuel. The heat is transferred from one stream of oil to the other by means of a heat exchanger.

The heat exchanger is of similar construction to the condenser already mentioned, but it handles two streams of oil instead of one (as vapour) and another of water. The side-

cuts also need cooling, and some of the heat which they give up can be used in the same way as that from the residue to warm up the crude oil feed.

The separation of fractions in this type of column is not complete; there is always some overlap between the boiling ranges of successive fractions. For instance, the kerosene may boil between 175 and 275°C and the gas oil between 225 and 350°C. This does not matter very much provided that the overlap is not too large. Apart from the column, pipestill and heat exchangers, most of the remaining space in a distillation unit is taken up with pumps, pipes and one small but vitally important building—the control room.

Oil refineries have for many years been pioneers of automatic control because of the great complexity of the processes which they use. To keep a large distillation unit running steadily, small adjustments to flow rates, pressures and temperatures are needed continuously. It would require far too many men to read the thermometers and flow-meters and gauges and make small changes on valve settings. Even if we had enough men, they would all be on a patch of ground perhaps 100 yards square, and some of them would have to be 100 feet up in the air at the top of columns. It would be quite impossible to co-ordinate their actions, so most of the controls arehautomated.

All flows, pressures and temperatures are measured by appropriate instruments and the readings are transmitted by electricity or compressed air to the control room, where they are displayed and recorded under the eye of the unit operator. In addition to informing the operator of conditions, many of these instruments control part of the process automatically. If, for example, there is any deviation from a set flow-rate, the instrument concerned can send a signal to the appropriate valve, which will then open or shut slightly so as to restore the flow to the desired rate. If the operator

13 *Crude oil distillation unit*

14 *Control room in a modern refinery. All units are controlled from this centre*

wishes to change the flow-rate, all he has to do is move the set point gently to the new value.

A modern process unit has large numbers of these recorders and controllers so that it can be run safely and steadily by only two or three men, and except when the unit is being started up and shut down, they do not have a great deal to do apart from seeing that all the instruments are acting normally.

Since the refinery runs day and night, 365 days a year, there will have to be several 'shift crews' for each control centre. All these men must know their job very thoroughly, so that they can detect immediately if anything goes wrong and take the correct action to keep the plant safe in an emergency. The only time the units are shut down in normal circumstances is about once every two years for a complete overhaul of all the equipment, including inspection of the insides of parts which cannot be seen when it is in use.

Distillation is the essential first stage in all oil refining and is also used in many other process units. Further, the automatic controls, pumps, heat exchangers, pipestills and many other bits of equipment turn up in different sizes in other processes.

9 · Improving the Products

The other refining processes which we need can be separated into 'sweetening', 'separation', and 'rebuilding'. Between them, they improve quality and enable us to balance the quantities of finished refined products.

The sweetening processes are concerned with the removal of sulphur to improve the smell of the products, to meet clean air requirements, and in the case of motor gasoline components to improve the effectiveness of tetra-ethyl lead addition. The lighter distillates, liquid petroleum gas, gasolines and kerosenes, can be sweetened by simple chemical treatments which either remove the sulphur compounds or turn them into relatively harmless and non-smelly forms. The simplest treatment of all uses a dilute solution of caustic soda in water; if this is insufficient, it may be fortified with other chemicals.

The process is simplicity itself—the oil and soda are mixed together and then allowed to separate. Separation is easy and the soda solution will settle out of the oil as it is passed through a large tank. A little more complicated to use, but effective with a rather wider range of distillates, especially if more sulphur must be removed, are processes using copper chloride or sulphuric acid or other specially developed chemical mixtures.

For gas oils, such methods would be ineffective or too expensive. The standard process now used for gas oil, and also suitable for light distillates, employs hydrogen over a catalyst at temperatures up to 400°C and pressures of 30 to 50 bar. A catalyst is a material which speeds up a chemical reaction without being changed itself. The one most used for desulphurisation is a mixture of oxides of cobalt, molybdenum and aluminium. A large unit may need 10 tons or more of this material. The high temperature and pressure of the process also demand special steels and welding for the pipes and reactor vessels. The metallurgist is an essential member of the teams who design such units.

After processing, the oil is clear and of good odour, but we also get as a by-product tons of stinking and dangerous hydrogen sulphide. Fortunately, this can be removed from the reaction products and converted to sulphur, for use in making sulphuric acid.

Some refineries use this desulphurisation process to treat a wide cut from gasoline up to kerosene or gas oil. The treated oil is redistilled to make cuts suitable for product blending. In each case the hydrogen must be supplied from other regular refinery processes or special units for hydrogen manufacture.

It is also possible, by using very severe pressure and temperature conditions, to use this type of process to reduce the sulphur content of residual fuel oils. Catalyst loses activity rapidly, fuel usage is large, and the equipment expensive. So far, few refineries outside the United States and Japan have needed such units, but they appear among possible choices for future processing worldwide.

Among the separation processes, distillation is the most important. It is the first essential even for the simplest refinery. We also use distillation to separate the special boiling point solvents from gasolines, to 'tailor' other cuts from crude oil for special uses, and to remove unwanted material from the products of the processes.

In the laboratory experiment described in the last chapter, it was shown that it was not possible to carry on distillation beyond about 350°C because there was then a tendency for the oil to break down or crack. However, we often want to distill crude oil beyond this temperature, especially in order to make the raw material for lubricating oil and certain other refining processes. To do this we make use of the fact that if we reduce the pressure, any liquid will boil at a temperature lower than its normal boiling point. This can be demonstrated in any laboratory with suitable glass equipment and a small ejector pump which can be run by tap water. The same principle is used in the refinery, except that the vacuum is usually obtained by steam ejectors. In this way the pressure inside a suitably designed column can be reduced to about one-tenth of normal atmospheric pressure or less.

Without using excessive pipestill temperatures, we can then distill off a material which at atmospheric pressure would boil in the range 350–550°C. This oil can be taken in several cuts if we wish, and is generally known as vacuum distillate. The residue from vacuum distillation is used for making bitumen and for some kinds of very viscous lubricating oil. Any left over from these products goes to fuel oil and is particularly useful to obtain very high viscosity fuel or improved low temperature fluidity. This last property may seem a little odd, but it results from the fact that most of the high melting point wax is contained in the vacuum distillates.

These variations on distillation do not exhaust the scope for separation processes. So far, heat has been necessary, but it is also possible to use cold, and separate various components from oil by crystallisation. This is especially important for extracting very pure aromatic compounds such as para-xylene, which is used in synthetic fibre manufacture. If we add a solvent to the oil and then chill the whole mixture, we have a useful method for removing wax from lubricating oils. Using solvents again, with controlled but not necessarily low temperatures, we have solvent extraction processes which are used in the manufacture of premium kerosene and high quality lubricating oils.

Solvent extraction works because some classes of hydrocarbon are more soluble than others in selected solvents. For example, aromatic compounds belonging to the same class as benzene and toluene are more soluble than are the paraffins and naphthenes in liquid sulphur dioxide. We want to get the aromatics out of premium kerosene because they burn with a dirty, smoky flame which is most objectionable in wick-fed lamps and heaters. So we arrange to mix the raw kerosene with liquid sulphur dioxide, pass it into a tall column (usually packed with earthenware rings inside, instead of the trays found in a distillation column) and allow the mixture to separate into two layers which are drawn off continuously at the top and bottom. The packing is there to ensure that the oil and sulphur dioxide, which normally enter the column separately, are really closely contacted as they flow through. One of the resulting layers is a solution of aromatics in sulphur dioxide, the other is mainly refined oil or raffinate, containing almost no aromatics and a relatively small amount of sulphur dioxide. Extract and raffinate are re-distilled in separate columns, and the sulphur dioxide is returned for re-use. The raffinate is given a final sweetening and is ready for use as premium kerosene. The extract can also be further refined and used in tractor vaporising oil and certain types of aromatic solvent.

Lubricating oil manufacture makes use of a variety of different solvent extractions, the choice depending on the preferences and economic considerations of the particular refinery. The object in the most important of these processes is to remove aromatics (once again) since these tend to make the oil rather thinner than we would like at high temperatures. Another important lubricating oil process which uses a solvent is the removal of asphalt from vacuum residue in the preparation of the more viscous grades. Strictly speaking, this is the precipitation of the asphalt from solution by the use of light hydrocarbon liquid. Before we have a finished lubricating oil, three or four separate processes may be necessary, and this accounts for its relatively high price.

This section of a big refinery is like a factory within a factory; indeed there are many small plants which specialize in this type of product. In addition to the refining processes, the lubricating oil section has to have its own installation for blending, barrelling and shipping the hundreds of different grades which different types of machinery require.

The rebuilding processes are most important to any refinery for improving quality, especially in motor gasolines, and for achieving the balance of product quantities required by the market. They also give the refiner some flexibility in meeting variations from season to season, beyond that which can be achieved by choosing crude oils giving different proportions of the principal fractions which we have discussed.

If oil is overheated it tends to break down chemically. But like many unwanted processes in nature, this can be turned to good account if ways of controlling it can be found. When distillate cuts from crude oil are heated strongly to about 500°C in a special pipestill, they can be broken down quite deliberately into lighter products. This process was first made use of some forty or fifty years ago to make more motor gasoline from the slightly heavier materials which were then in less demand. The cracking is not complete, and there is some residue left over which must be absorbed in fuel oils. Gasoline made in this way contains a high proportion of olefins (unsaturated hydrocarbons with less than their full quota of hydrogen), which have improved anti-knock quality. Because the olefins are more reactive than paraffins boiling in the same range, there is also a tendency to form undesirable gums, but we have additives which will suppress this type of reaction. For various reasons, thermal cracking is not much used now for gasoline manufacture, but a variation of the process is used to make ethylene and propylene for petrochemical manufacture.

In the middle 1930's, research workers in the industry found a process much better than thermal cracking for making extra high quality gasoline. This involves bringing the hot feedstock into contact with a catalyst consisting mainly of oxides of aluminium and silicon. By careful selection of the feedstock, precise type of catalyst and temperature for reaction, it is possible to convert well over half the feed into motor spirit components and be left with only a small amount of heavy high-boiling oil. The favoured feedstock for catalytic cracking is vacuum distillate or the higher-boiling material from the gas oil range. Using this sort of process we can take material which would normally have to go into fuel oil, and convert it into the more valuable motor spirit, obtaining a high quality component for good measure. In a market such as North America, which requires a much higher proportion of motor gasoline components than could be distilled direct from any crude oil, this is especially valuable.

The process as originally developed had one major

drawback; some of the feedstock is converted to carbon and remains stuck to the catalyst, whose activity is quickly lost. Activity can be restored by passing air through the catalyst while it is still hot and burning the carbon off, but this involves having several small reactors and using each in turn while the catalyst in the others is 'regenerated'. Units like this were not at all convenient to operate, so another means of regeneration was sought.

The later type of unit uses a very finely ground catalyst, so fine that it behaves in many ways like a liquid. This 'fluid' catalyst is drawn off continuously from the reactor vessel and blown into a regenerator by the air needed to burn the carbon off the catalyst particles. The catalyst, freshened up, is drawn off from the regenerator and carried back into the reactor by a hot stream of oil feed. A big 'cat. cracker' may contain 200 tons or more of fluid catalyst. The products after separation from the catalyst are led away to distillation columns where they are sorted into cuts suitable for motor gasoline and other finished products.

In photograph no. 15 you will see very large structures like tall cylinders. These are the reactor and the regenerator (the latter with the chimney stack on top). Some cat. crackers have these two vessels one on top of the other instead of side by side, but the process inside is just the same. All the rest of the unit consists of distillation equipment, pumps, compressors and other machinery, plus a small fired heater.

The next important rebuilding process which is in widespread use is the catalytic reformer, and these have been used in refineries since about 1950. Once again, a catalyst is needed, this time a very expensive one containing from a half to one percent of platinum. A large unit could need about 20 tons of this catalyst. It operates at high temperatures, above 500°C, and at pressures usually in the range of 30 to 50 bar. The cat. reformer does a very different job from

15 *Catalytic cracker unit*

the cat. cracker, although both are concerned with making high grade motor gasoline. The cat. reformer takes a heavy gasoline boiling in the 80–180°C range and its main task is to improve the octane number. It does this by removing hydrogen from the naphthenic hydrocarbons and thus converting them into aromatics which have much better knock-ratings. Some of the paraffins are cracked, or become altered in structure; these changes also improve the octane number, and produce some lighter material so that the product has very nearly the boiling range required for a finished motor spirit.

The process as a whole turns up a surplus of hydrogen, which is separated from the rest of the reaction products. Part is returned to the reactors, since the catalyst only works properly in the presence of excess hydrogen; the remainder is exactly what is needed to run the catalytic desulphurisation units. As with all catalytic processes, the heart of the unit is the reactor vessels, large drums made of special steel with walls over 25 mm thick to stand the pressure within. Large pipestill heaters are also needed, and space for the distillation columns and pumps and pipes common to all refinery units; one somewhat unusual feature which cat. reformers share with desulphurisation units and some other catalytic processes is the possession of very large compressors for recirculating hydrogen to the reactors.

Cat. crackers and cat. reformers both make considerable quantities of light hydrocarbon gases with from one to four carbon atoms. The cat. reformer gives methane, ethane, propane and butane, but the cracker gases also contain a high proportion of the olefinic gases ethylene, propylene, and various forms of butane. Some part of this surplus gas can of course be sold as liquid gas or burnt in the refinery. But it is also possible to use further catalytic processes to recombine some of these gases into gasoline-range liquids, and once

16   *Catalytic reforming unit*

again these gasolines have exceptionally good anti-knock properties.

One of these processes is polymerisation, and for this we pass olefin rich gas from the cat. cracker at high temperature and pressure over a catalyst containing phosphoric acid. The resulting product is known as polymer gasoline, and requires only the removal of excess propane and butane to leave it in a form suitable for motor spirit blending.

The other main process of this kind requires olefin gases from the cat. cracker together with gas from the cat. reformer, which is rich in the form of butane for which the chemists' name is iso-butane. These materials are reacted together in the presence of concentrated sulphuric acid or hydrofluoric acid. This time, the gasoline contains very little olefinic material, unlike the polymer gasoline, but is very rich in iso-octane. The importance of iso-octane is that it is one of the best hydrocarbons for knock-rating and the product of this 'Alkylation' process is an essential ingredient in the high-performance gasolines for piston-engined aircraft, besides being useful for ordinary motor spirits.

It is desirable to be able to convert the maximum amount of residue and heavy distillate to higher valued products such as gasoline, petrochemical feedstock and jet fuel. Most United States refiners already have such capability, and elsewhere it will be wanted on a larger scale than at present. Further processes which can be used include hydrocracking and coking (in the latter some of the product can be in the form of metallurgical coke). The right choice of process and operating conditions give some freedom to the refiner to select the type of product output needed.

10 · The Refinery

The central feature of the refinery is its process units—distillation, cracking, reforming, desulphurisation, and whatever else has been judged necessary for the manufacture of its particular range of products. The process area can be identified by the tall distillation columns and chimneys for fired heaters. The process units occupy only a relatively small part of the total ground area. Much the largest area is taken up by storage tanks for crude oil and products in various stages of manufacture. Some of the tanks look as if they have no tops. The roofs are there in fact, but they are designed to float up and down as the tanks are filled and emptied. This is necessary with crude oil and the more volatile products such as gasoline, so as to reduce loss of vapour and to control the fire hazard which would exist if large amounts of inflammable vapour were allowed to drift around. A few of the smaller tanks will contain fuel oil which the refinery needs to run its own fired heaters. (Oil and gas used for furnaces within the refinery may account for 5 percent or more of the total crude oil brought in.)

Blending of finished products will be done at some place within the tankage area, or tank farm, as it is commonly called. Some products can be ready in their finished form direct from a refinery process unit; all that has to be done is pump them away to tanks where they await delivery to the company's other storage depots or to the customer. But many products are made by blending together several refined oils, possibly from a variety of process units. Motor gasoline is a good illustration of this. It can take anything from two up to five or six components, plus tetraethyl lead fluid and any other dyes and additives which the company has decided to use. This, incidentally, gives us further scope for balancing overall product requirements, since there are usually a variety of blends which will give the desired quality, and we also have the opportunity of varying the quality of items such as cat. reformer gasoline during manufacture. Motor spirit is about the most complicated product in this respect, but many others use two or more components to achieve the final product quality required.

In the older type of refinery, this blending is done by pumping the appropriate amount of each component from its own tank into a large finished product tank (which might hold anything from a few hundred up to 30,000 tons of oil). The contents are then well mixed, usually by drawing off oil from the tank and pumping it back through a special inlet designed to help mixing.

Refineries built in the last few years have tended to use a different system, in which the components are mixed in the correct proportions within a pipeline, under the eye of an automatic controller. The blend so made may be pumped directly into a cross-country pipeline or aboard the ship which is to deliver it; this type of operation is increasingly common. The accuracy and reliability of the instruments which control the method of blending clearly has to be very

17 *The 400 hectare site of the Fawley oil refinery*

good, and it is only within quite recent time that we have had good enough equipment at a price which makes it an attractive alternative to traditional blending by tank mixing.

Whatever method of blending is used, no product leaves the refinery without testing to ensure that it matches the quality specified. To this end, every refinery has a laboratory to perform physical and chemical tests which are standardized throughout the industry. Laboratories have to be prepared to work twenty-four hours a day, like everything else in the refinery, since the manufacture, blending and movement of oil is a continuous process. The laboratory building always used to be separate from other offices, but in the modern compact type of refinery it may be under the same roof as the administrative offices and a central control room from which the entire refinery is operated.

Once the products have been made and tested, they must be sent away to the customers. Storage tanks are expensive to build and there is no special merit in keeping very large stocks of all grades of product within the refinery. So far as possible, blends are made up and sent away as required. Small amounts will be kept in constant readiness for those grades which are moved regularly every day by road and rail or by barges and coasters. To get the products away there must be jetties for tankers and barges if the refinery is near the sea or on the banks of a large river. There must also be loading places for road and rail tank cars, and pumping stations if the oil is to be despatched by pipeline. All the loading places must of course be connected to the tanks by pumps and pipes. For convenience, the pipes run as far as possible together in special pipe-tracks which may be as wide as a large main road.

Refineries are large consumers of steam and electricity, so they need large boilers. Sometimes these are now built into the process units so as to make the best use of waste heat. If

18 *Operating a sphere launcher
at the pumping station of a multi-product pipeline*

the refinery needs to generate its own electricity, the boilers will be housed in a central power station. The power station will be very much like any other, and may be big enough to look after the needs of a fair-sized town. Having used heat for many of the essential processes, provision must be made for cooling the products down again before they go into the tanks. A really large refinery may need many thousands of cubic metres of water every hour for coolers and condensers in the process units. Water is expensive in these quantities because it costs money in pumping even if it can be drawn out of the sea.

At an inland refinery, there may simply not be enough water, and in addition there is always some risk of the waste water becoming contaminated with oil. There are means of stopping contamination, but this involves still more special equipment. Accordingly, many new refineries are cooled by air, using fans rather like gigantic car radiators.

Big refineries always have a large engineering staff to overhaul machinery and process plant. Smaller refineries may rely on outside help to do their major overhauls, but even they must have some engineers and mechanics to do the everyday jobs in keeping the plant running smoothly. There must also be stores for spare parts and chemicals, and there must be the office staff to administer and plan the whole operation. This work calls for people trained in all sorts of trades and professions. There may be only 100 workers in a small or simply arranged refinery, but there can be up to 2,000 in a big and complex plant, especially if it was built a few years ago before the recent big spurt in developing automatic control equipment.

Even a small refinery may be handling a million tons of oil a year, and perhaps one of the most remarkable things about it is the small number of men who can be seen around during normal operations. This is a measure of the industry's success in applying automatic operation, which keeps down costs and keeps up quality and reliability in what is perhaps the most highly technical large industry in the world today.

11 · Moving Oil Around the World – Tankers

The world needs nearly 6 million tons of oil products every single day, and this vast amount is growing rapidly. Every drop of this must be ready for use at the right time, at the right place, in the correct quantity, in a suitable quality, and at a price which is both acceptable to the user and profitable to the oil company which sells it. All of it must be moved at least twice, from the oil well to the refinery, and from the refinery to the user, and often this movement will have to be in several stages.

Oil is moved by water in ships of all sizes, by road and rail, and through pipelines, the method being chosen to suit the quantity to be moved and the distance between source and the intended delivery point. In every case the cheapest feasible form of transport must be chosen so as to keep the cost to the customer as low as possible.

Perhaps the least known and certainly the least glamorized of all forms of oil transport are the little ships. All around our coasts and on the great inland waterways of

19 *Barge train on Seine River, France*

America, and all over Europe, there are whole fleets of barges and coasters which can carry from 100 to as much as 3,000 tons of oil at a time. They fill up at refineries and large depots on the coasts and rivers, and supply smaller depots and large factories with oil products of all descriptions. They slide quietly in and out of small ports almost unnoticed, fulfilling their vital part in the movement of oil.

The barges are indeed almost invisible when fully loaded; they are designed to work in sheltered water, so they need little free-board and sail with their decks almost awash. These little ships, like their big sisters, are almost all oil tank. Virtually the whole of the hull apart from the machinery space is used for carrying their liquid cargo. The main part of the hull is divided up into several compartments—from two to about twelve, depending on the size of the ship. This enables them to carry several different grades of oil. It also ensures that if the weather is rough, or the ship is not completely full, the oil will not slop around and upset the trim of the ship. These small ships must also have pumps and pipes so that the oil can be directed to the correct tanks at loading, and discharged at its destination without help from the shore, apart from hoses to connect with the depot pipes.

The big ocean-going tankers are simply huge versions of the small coasters, with the difference that they are designed

20 *Coastal tanker discharging products in Turkey*

to travel long distances through any kind of sea and carry extremely large quantities of oil. All these ocean tankers are built to a common pattern, regardless of size, which may range from 10,000 to 500,000 dead-weight tons (dwt for short).

The term 'dead-weight tons' is always used to describe the size of tankers. It refers to the carrying capacity for cargo plus fuel and other essential stores. The cargo capacity will be at least nine-tenths of the dwt measurement, more in the case of the larger classes of tanker.

As in small tankers, the hull of the big ones is divided into compartments, of which there may be from fifteen to over forty. The divisions are made by bulkheads running across the ship and along its length. Usually there are two lengthwise bulkheads, so each of the tanks running across the ship is divided into three compartments, port, centre and starboard. The centre one is the largest. There may be ten or more tanks, numbered from bow to stern. At perhaps two points in the length of the ship there are 'cofferdams' which are like narrow tanks running across the ship. They house the pumps and other machinery needed for unloading the oil from the ship. The cargo tanks use up most of the space in the hull. The extreme bow space is used for the tanker's own fuel and for other heavy stores. The machinery space for the main engines is always in the stern, so that the propeller shaft can be kept short and does not have to pass through the cargo tanks in a separate tunnel.

The main engines may be either diesels or steam turbines. In the latter case, there have to be big boilers to raise steam for the turbines. Whatever sort of main engine is chosen, there will be small diesel-driven electric generators. Most tankers, even the largest, have only one propeller, though this may be driven through a gigantic gearbox, from more than one turbine.

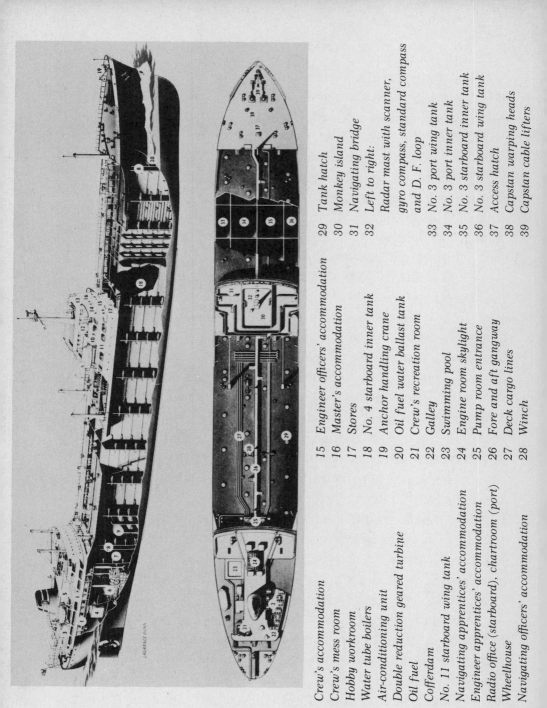

1   Crew's accommodation
2   Crew's mess room
3   Hobby workroom
4   Water tube boilers
5   Air-conditioning unit
6   Double reduction geared turbine
7   Oil fuel
8   Cofferdam
9   No. 11 starboard wing tank
10 Navigating apprentices' accommodation
11 Engineer apprentices' accommodation
12 Radio office (starboard), chartroom (port)
13 Wheelhouse
14 Navigating officers' accommodation
15 Engineer officers' accommodation
16 Master's accommodation
17 Stores
18 No. 4 starboard inner tank
19 Anchor handling crane
20 Oil fuel water ballast tank
21 Crew's recreation room
22 Galley
23 Swimming pool
24 Engine room skylight
25 Pump room entrance
26 Fore and aft gangway
27 Deck cargo lines
28 Winch
29 Tank hatch
30 Monkey island
31 Navigating bridge
32 Left to right:
     Radar mast with scanner,
     gyro compass, standard compass
     and D. F. loop
33 No. 3 port wing tank
34 No. 3 port inner tank
35 No. 3 starboard inner tank
36 No. 3 starboard wing tank
37 Access hatch
38 Capstan warping heads
39 Capstan cable lifters

Fig. 6   *Sectional view of an ocean-going tanker*

21 *The 249,542 dwt* Esso Scotia

In older tankers, the living and working space for the crew is usually in two parts—a centrecastle which includes the bridge from which the ship is navigated, and cabins and living-rooms for the officers and perhaps some deck-hands, and an aftercastle over the engine room housing the rest of the crew. The most modern ships are nearly all of 'all-aft' construction, with no centrecastle. This has two advantages; it reduces the total size and weight of superstructure, and it puts all the officers and crew together so that nobody has to cross the open deck while the ship is at sea. Navigation becomes a little more difficult, especially when docking or manoeuvering in narrow waters, because the visibility from the stern is not as good as from the centre of the ship. Some tankers have been fitted with closed-circuit television cameras in the bows and a screen on the bridge, so that the navigating officer can see what is going on just ahead of the ship when she is coming alongside jetties or making other difficult movements.

The service speed of most tankers is not much over 30 km/h. This may seem slow compared with the 50 km/h of the 'Queens' or even with the 35 to 45 km/h of the majority of other passenger liners. The reason for the more modest speeds of tankers is economy. It takes a lot of extra power to get an extra kilometre/h out of a ship, and the fact that they work for an oil company does not mean that the fuel is free. If the tankers did not use it, it could be sold to someone else, so the tanker-operating company pays just like any other customer.

The crews of tankers are quite small—about thirty to forty is common for modern ships—and vary little with the size of the ship, once out of the small coaster class. The small numbers are made possible by having as many operations as possible, especially in the engine room, carried out automatically or by remote control from a central control room.

The principles and means are much the same as those used for control of a process unit in a refinery. Accommodation for the crew in a modern tanker is of the highest standard, with good cabins and messrooms, and the larger vessels even have swimming pools. This is not a waste of the owners' money. Tankers are not altogether convenient ships to work on, since they often do long voyages, never spend much time in port, and for safety reasons there have to be rigid rules about such things as smoking on board. So to get and keep experienced crew, some compensations must be offered.

The smaller ocean tankers, up to about 20,000 dwt, are used mainly for carrying products from refineries to the oil companies' ocean terminals and to very large industrial customers whose works are near the sea and who can take thousands of tons of oil at a time. The useful size is limited because product carriers may have to work into relatively small ports, and the amount of tankage into which they can discharge may also be limited. Product tankers may take a full cargo of one grade of oil, but frequently they have to carry several grades on the same voyage. The greatest care must then be taken to ensure that things do not get mixed on board or while pumping them in or out of the ship.

These tankers are commonly divided into 'clean' and 'dirty,' or 'white' and 'black'. The black or dirty vessels carry only residual fuel oil or sometimes crude oil. The others may carry any other product. Black vessels are difficult to clean out, because the fuels they carry are dark-coloured and viscous and would contaminate and discolour any other products. So the owners will not wish to waste valuable time cleaning them for a white cargo unless this is the only way of keeping the ship usefully employed. The reverse change is easier, but care must be taken to ensure that no traces of volatile products are left on board, since they could lower the flash point (the temperature at which the oil tends to catch fire) and make the residual fuel less safe to handle. Occasionally, larger ships are used for products, but this depends on the receiving terminal being able to handle them, so this is not a very common occurrence.

The biggest ships are used almost entirely for carrying crude oil. A few refineries are sited near oilfields, or can be fed from oilfields by direct pipeline. The majority, outside of the United States at least, have to be supplied by sea, although the journey may start or finish in a long distance pipeline. It is not as a rule too difficult to arrange for a refinery in Europe to have a crude oil terminal situated on a deep-water anchorage. A refinery will have to take in between half a million and perhaps 25 million tons of crude oil a year.

As a general rule, the larger the cargo, the cheaper it will be per ton to transport it. This is because tanker costs do not go up in direct proportion to the size of the vessel. A consequence of this is that a long voyage for a really big tanker may be cheaper, per ton again, than a shorter voyage for a smaller ship. The voyage from the Arabian Gulf to Europe has to be undertaken by hundreds of tankers every year, but it is economic to build very large ships which could not possibly go through the Suez Canal and have to go right round South Africa instead. The ones which could use the Canal are simply more expensive to use. Accordingly although there are still many crude oil tankers of 30,000–50,000 dwt in use, oil companies are now having mammoth tankers built in sizes up to 500,000 dwt.

Even larger tankers than this have been considered, but they have special problems which may prevent their widespread use, quite apart from the technical difficulties of building and sailing them. The ports where the giants can load and discharge are few, since they may draw more than 20 m of water when fully loaded. They can even produce difficulties about the routes they can use when anywhere near land—few of the United States' East Coast ports for instance are deep enough. Some companies have sought to solve the problem of unloading at a deep-water port into rather smaller ships which can reach their refineries safely. Several very large crude oil depots are now in use in Europe for this purpose. Others have solved the problem by transferring oil between tankers while still at sea but in fairly sheltered water.

These tankers are not by any means all owned by the oil companies. Although the larger companies do own a lot of the ships they need, they tend not to have more than the minimum number to which they can give fulltime employment. Any others they require are hired from independent owners who specialize in shipping. These owners may have a whole fleet of tankers, like some of the Greek shipping magnates, or they may have only a few as part of a general cargo fleet. Either way, the ships are taken on hire, or chartered, by the oil companies. Sometimes the hiring may be for a period of months or years ('time charter'), otherwise the ships may be taken on 'voyage charter' for one or two trips to fill a gap in an oil company's immediate needs.

Any day of the year, there are millions of tons of oil being carried around the world in ocean tankers. Occasionally, oil gets spilt. This may be the result of an accident—a collision at sea, or a ship going aground—or it may be the result of sheer carelessness in disposing of water used for ballast or in cleaning out tanks. (It is fair to mention here that tankers are not the only vessels to blame; other large ships also carry oil, as fuel, and may be less than careful over what they do with the residues from cleaning out their tanks.) The oil companies and the independent tanker owners are very much aware that their vessels may spill oil and cause pollution of the sea and sea-coasts. International agreements are slowly being brought into effect to stop any vessel from discharging oil where it might cause danger or damage. Offenders can be fined—heavily—and eventually we should be able to stop pollution caused by lack of care or by bad planning.

Collisions and groundings, however, are less easy to prevent. There have been a number of serious accidents on or near North American shores in recent years. One of the worst, in terms of the amount of oil involved, was the grounding and eventual break-up in December, 1976, of the Liberian tanker *Argo Merchant* on the Nantucket Shoals. The entire cargo of 5,000,000 tons of heavy industrial fuel oil was spilled into the Atlantic Ocean, endangering the New England coast, as well as the Georges Bank, one of the world's richest commercial fishing areas. Nor are ships the only cause of such disasters. A blow-out on an offshore drilling platform in California's Santa Barbara Channel in 1969 resulted in huge amounts of oil going ashore. In every case there has been great immediate loss of life among seabirds and among the animals and plants living between the high and low tide marks on the shore. Cleaning up the beaches to prevent more damage and to make them accept-able once again to visitors and to the local population is a gigantic task. The Santa Barbara incident alone is estimated to have cost $5 million.

As a result of such disasters, much has been learned about how to minimise the effects. The best thing is undoubtedly to skim up the oil before it reaches the shore, and a number of machines have been devised to do this. If the sea is too rough for skimming, oil can be dispersed and diluted in the water with the aid of chemicals. When it is properly dispersed, the oil is slowly destroyed by air and bacteria—nature helping man out of troubles of his own making. Once ashore, oil is very difficult to deal with. To restore the amenity of sandy beaches, the oil can be cleared

22 *Thousands of birds may suffer after an oil spill at sea*

with shovels and bulldozers, helped with absorbent materials where possible. Elsewhere it is usually best left to nature, since the damage to wildlife can be made worse by dispersing the oil over a wider range. Nature is remarkably efficient. In every case examined by expert biologists the damage has started to repair itself within a matter of months, with new colonies of plants and animals moving in to settle on the damaged areas. Complete restoration may take years, but always seems to work provided that there is no further spill of oil and that rare species have not been endangered.

12 · Moving Oil
– Transport Over Land

The most familiar sort of oil transport must be the road tank car. In America they commonly have capacities between 20 and 40 tons, though smaller ones are also to be seen. Sizes are limited by state law. In Europe, and especially in Britain, road cars tend to be smaller, mainly because the road systems in the older towns and villages will not cope with big vehicles, and some bridges take only limited loads. In any country they are a familiar sight at service stations, dropping their loads of motor spirit for sale to the private motorist.

They are also widely used for the delivery of many other products to factories and large customers whose needs suit this size of transport or who do not have access for anything else. The tank car's load may have been picked up at a refinery or at a smaller depot which is kept filled from a refinery by other types of transport. Road tank cars may also be used to keep depots filled up if this happens to be the most convenient way of doing it; this kind of operation is often known as a 'bridging run'. Usually, however, since road

118

transport is expensive in manpower and equipment, it is used only where deliveries are reasonably small or it is not possible to use anything else.

Anyone who lives near a railway must also have seen rail tank wagons carrying oil products. The smallest ones carry a similar amount to the larger road tank cars, in the region of 10 tons. The larger wagons carry up to 90 tons each. This size has long been common in America, and is increasingly used in Europe. Rail tank wagons are used to a considerable extent for deliveries to factories which have rail sidings, and to supply the oil companies' own inland depots. For the latter job particularly, it is increasingly common practice to make up whole trains of oil wagons to run regularly from a refinery to a single depot. Several different types of product can be taken by one train, but it is not usually possible to load

23   *Detail view of a road tank car*

different things in the same tank wagon, although this is often done with road tank cars, which are fitted with a number of separate compartments. Most road and rail tankers can only discharge the load by running it out under gravity, or with the assistance of a fixed pump which is part of the depot or factory equipment.

Pipes and pumps have been used regularly over the past hundred years for moving oil from wells to places where it can be put into other forms of transport, and over distances of a few miles to refineries, at least since the time that the quantities became too large to handle conveniently in barrels. Moving oil over really long distances by pipelines became possible when the necessary large capacity high pressure pumps and suitable steel pipe became safe, cheap and reliable. Long distance pipelines have been in use for over sixty years, and hardly a year passes without something still more spectacular being tackled, in the way of distance or amount of oil to be moved. There are now many long distance crude oil pipeline systems in North America, several in North Africa and the Middle East, and an increasing number in Europe to serve inland refineries.

As an example, consider how crude oil can be moved from the new fields on the North Slope of Alaska. There is no local market and all the oil, amounting to over 50 million tons every year, must be moved out to places where it can be refined. The shallow ice-bound Arctic coast is no place to take conventional oil tankers. The solution is to pump the oil through a pipeline some 1300 km from Prudhoe Bay to Valdez and load it to tankers in an ice-free port on onward movement to the refining and marketing centres of the West Coast. The pipe diameter is 1.2 metres; there are few others as large as this. In such lines a pumping pressure of 60 bar is commonly used, but even this will not move oil at the desired rate over the huge distances involved, so extra pumping stations are installed to boost up the pressure for successive stages of the journey. A major problem in Alaska has been to insulate the line so that the oil remains warm enough to flow readily and so that lost heat does not melt the frozen icy soil.

High pressure pipelines are also used to move natural gas and all kinds of liquid oil products from their source at well or refinery into the areas where they are to be used. Pumping the same sort of crude oil or gas continuously down a line, from storage tanks at one end to tanks at the receiving depot, is a fairly straightforward operation. Pumping a series of different products presents some extra problems, since it is most important that they should not get mixed during their journey. In fact, provided that the flow rate is suitably controlled, mixing at the 'interface' between products is not very great. The pipeline operators arrange the sequence of products so that a small amount of contamination between one and the next will not be absolutely ruinous to the quality of either.

There is still the problem of finding the interface when it arrives at the receiving end of the line. The simplest way of doing this is to measure how much oil has been put in, and make sure that you get the same amount out again; but it is essential to remember that in this case you are entirely dependent on the precision of flow measurements and must ensure that due account is taken of expansion or contraction due to temperature difference between the two ends of the line. It is also possible to measure continuously some property of the oil, such as its density, at the point of arrival at the receiving terminal. It is not even necessary to know exactly what the density of the oil is supposed to be, or make any temperature correction, because any sudden change will show that the next product in the pumping programme has arrived. The incoming flow can then be diverted from one tank to another by opening and closing the appropriate valves, either by hand or automatically on a signal from the density recorder.

A third way of checking what is going on in a pipeline is to insert some solid separator at the interface, fitting closely enough in the pipe to make sure that it will be pushed along at the same rate as the oil. Such devices are known as 'batching pigs'. They can be arranged to trigger off an alarm or start automatic valve changes as they arrive at their destination, just as a density recorder signal can be used for this purpose. 'Pigs' are inserted and withdrawn from the line through a set of double doors on a short extension at either end. They are used for other purposes besides separation of products, too, notably for cleaning the insides of lines to keep them free from rust and from the waxy deposits which may settle out from crude and fuel oils.

The progress of a pig along a pipeline can be followed by listening for it with a kind of primitive stethoscope, and hearing the squeal which it makes against the walls of the pipe especially when it goes round bends. It is also possible to fit the pig with a radio-active capsule and follow it with a Geiger counter from outside the line. This is more satisfactory, though more expensive, since it gives an accurate method of locating the pig should it get stuck in the line—a distinct possibility for a cleaning pig.

Pipes are usually laid underground and indeed this is quite essential in country where there are many roads and fields and other obstacles to cross. It is very often done in open country as well, mainly as a protection against extremes of temperature and accidental damage. Special digging machinery is needed, and equipment for welding the pipe sections together and laying them into the trench. Lines can be laid across astonishingly rough country, the route being limited partly by considerations of power needed for pumping and partly by feasibility of access for the pipe-laying machinery.

Pipelines are expensive to lay, especially if they have to traverse many natural or man-made obstacles. Nor are they particularly cheap to operate, since they need large pumps to keep the oil flowing and the lines themselves need a certain amount of attention to keep them protected from corrosion by water and minerals in the soil. More important still, a pipeline is a fixed route once it has been laid, and cannot be moved. So it is generally used only if there are special circumstances which would make other forms of transport even more expensive, if it has work guaranteed for a long time ahead, and if it can be kept in use at near full capacity all the time.

We have now looked at all the major ways of transporting

24   *Plastic pig used to clean a 750 mm diameter pipeline in Libya*

oil, leaving out only barrels and cans which are never used except for very small deliveries or for destinations where it is quite impossible to use anything else. Broadly speaking, pipelines and ocean tankers are used to move large quantities of crude oil to refineries, and for deliveries of products to large storage depots and major customers like power stations, steelworks or petrochemical factories. Smaller ships move products from refineries or main depots to smaller distribution centres or customers' works which happen to be in ports or beside canals and rivers. Road and rail wagons are used for all the remaining deliveries where quite small amounts are all that is needed.

There are two special forms of final delivery to users which demand some further mention—aircraft fuelling and ship bunkering. A large airliner such as a Boeing 707 or a VC-10 has a fuel tank capacity of about 90,000 litres or 80 tons; the 'jumbo-jets' like the Boeing 747 will take nearly twice this amount when fuelling for a flight at maximum range. The fuelling company must be prepared to put this on board in about half an hour if the flight is not to be delayed— a very high rate if you think of how long it takes to put a few litres into the family car.

There are two ways of tackling this. The first is to bring alongside one or more special large-capacity road tank cars, fitted with their own pumps (and the filters we mentioned before). These are connected up to the aircraft by means of hoses about 65 mm in diameter.

The other system is to have a hydrant (like a fire main, but full of aviation fuel instead of water) with branches to the aircraft parking spaces round the airport. A small trailer carrying a filter is brought up and connected between the hydrant and the aircraft by hoses. The pumps in this case are at the airfield fuel tankage area. As in all operations where

25 *Welding a pipeline in mountainous country, Austria*

oil is handled, the most stringent precautions are taken to ensure that fire cannot be started by sparks, electrical discharges, or the careless use of naked lights such as matches. By these means, millions of tons of fuel are put aboard aircraft all over the world each year in complete safety.

Every port must be able to deliver fuel to the ships which visit it, and most nowadays use oil in some form. Near the harbour or docks you will therefore find tank farms which hold supplies of the residual fuel and diesel oil which ships need. Small craft and coasters may be fuelled from a road tank car which drives on to the quay. Bigger ships, because of the amount they need, must have their supply from a

26 *(opposite)*   *Tankers loading at Puerto Miranda, Venezuela*

27 *(below)*   *Shell lighter bunkering a Russian merchant ship*

pipeline connected to the tank farm with its tanks and pumps. An ocean liner may want several thousand tons of oil for a long voyage, and to keep its stay in port as short as possible the owners and the master will want this pumped aboard at several hundred tons an hour. Some harbours are too shallow to bring ships alongside the quays, and then it is necessary for the pipeline to run out along the sea-bed to a small island—it may be a floating one—from which oil is taken up to the ship through large flexible hoses in the usual way.

The idea of anchoring ships some way off shore to load bunkers is often extended to loading and unloading crude oil cargoes for big tankers. This saves the cost of jetties and special dredging to make a channel up to the shore.

28   *Bow mooring device which enables large tankers to be loaded under any weather conditions*

13 · Planning the Supply of Oil

Selling gasoline and lubricating oil for cars and central-heating oil to houses may be quite a small part of an oil company's total activity, though it is certainly a very vital part. As with all big businesses, much of the oil is sold wholesale, in large quantities, to big users or to other firms to market. A deal in fuel oil may go on for years and involve millions of tons. All the information on what products have been sold, where and when they are to be delivered, and what quality is required, must be sent to a central supply organization. The job of this part of the firm is to arrange for deliveries, in conjunction with the departments which know all about oilfields and crude oil supplies, about refineries, and about transport which the firm owns or can charter.

It is not very difficult to work out what is wanted tomorrow, or even next month, but someone has also got to decide what is likely to be required in five years' time. Not many contracts are fixed so far ahead, but if there are any, they will probably be very large and important and the firm must be prepared to meet them.

Estimates must be made of the likely quantity and quality needed by the markets for all of the company's products for some time ahead, and consideration given to whether any new kinds of products should be made and sold. These estimates will influence decisions on refining and shipping capacity which may not even be built yet, and neither of these things can be provided overnight. Estimates of this kind about the company's future activities must also take account of oil well production—some fields will be expanded, some may even run dry in the course of five years. The planners therefore must be thinking well into the future, and continually revise their estimates as more and better information about future needs becomes available. Revision is important since world demand exceeds 2.5 billion tons per year, and an error of even one percent in estimating the rate of growth represents a huge amount of oil.

A large oil company will have many sources of crude oil, some of which it may own, others of which it may expect to make use of by buying from another organization. It will have a nubmer of refineries, perhaps several in one country with others scattered around more than one continent. It will also serve a variety of market areas, each needing a diversity of products. Each of these market areas must be served at the least possible cost to the company. It is always true that if a company does not sell its wares and make some profit out of the activity there will be no money to spend on expansion, and eventually the business will collapse under pressure from its competitors.

It is of course possible to work out the best way of using all the company resources to supply the required products in each market area at the least possible cost. The calculations, however, become extremely complex and there will be an enormous number of possible solutions, some of them better than others. The difference between a reasonable answer and the best one may be worth a great deal of money.

In recent years the major oil companies have been among the pioneers in the use of electronic computers to solve supply problems. The computer must be supplied with the best possible information on the quantities and qualities of products needed, the capacity and costs of refineries and ships available to the company, the availability of crude oil, and a variety of other things. All this must be done in the form of mathematical equations, and we can then instruct the computer how to solve these equations so as to fulfill the whole production plan at the least cost. The machine will be instructed to work in such a way that each successive answer will be better than the one before, and eventually it will print out in plain words and figures the best possible answer to the problem as set. There is of course always the possibility of giving inaccurate information or poor instructions on how to solve the problem, and it could come up with some pretty fatuous answers.

Sooner or later, human judgment must be used on whether to accept the solution as given by the computer, or reject it and look for faults in the information or the operation of the machine. Computer solutions to supply problems are now the basis, in many oil companies, for the day-to-day instructions to oilfields, refineries and transport services. They help us to meet rapidly growing and changing demands for oil products in the most efficient possible way.

14 · People in the Oil Industry

A large oil company, with activities in exploration and crude oil production, refining, transportation, sales and research, requires a staff which will run to tens of thousands, and will include people with an enormous diversity of trades, professions and special skills. The balance will vary greatly from one company to another, depending on where they operate and which activities are of the greatest importance to them.

The oil industry needs very large amounts of money invested in ships, plant and mechanical equipment, and once it has these things it needs relatively small numbers of people to run them and achieve a very large output of products. Small is a relative term, and because the industry and many of the companies in it are among the biggest in the world, the numbers of people involved can be very considerable.

The first on the scene when an area is selected for oil exploration are the geologists and geophysicists. Their job is to map the sub-surface rocks and make recommendations on

132

29 *Geologist collecting rock samples in the Canadian Rockies*

the places where oil might be found. The leaders at least, in an exploration party, must be university-trained earth scientists with considerable experience in this type of work. They will be assisted by other geologists and by experts in fossils and rock composition, by map-makers and surveyors. From time to time they will have to call on outside help, especially when aerial surveys have to be made, since it is unusual for an oil company to keep its own aircraft and pilots for this sort of work. The oil geologist has to be prepared for a roving life. Most of the well-developed countries have been extensively surveyed, and the interest of the companies extends to very remote parts, like the icy wastes of Alaska, the jungles of Central Africa, and deserts of the Middle East, N. Africa and Australia, and under shallower parts of the seas.

When the geologists have done their work, and if they have found likley places for oil accumulations under the ground, the drillers move in. For this work the leader will be a specialist engineer whose working life has been devoted to making holes in the ground. He will direct a drillig crew, who, though they need not be professionally qualified engineers, will mostly be highly skilled men who have acquired their knowledge on the job. They also must be prepared to work in remote places, possibly for months at a stretch, and then perhaps to move to another job on the far side of the world. The work can be dangerous at times, the more so since in recent years more and more drilling has been done in the shallower parts of the oceans. Most of their work is done once the size of a new oilfield has been defined and the necessary production wells are complete. Some of them will have to stay on to help keep the wells working and in good condition for maximum production.

When sufficient wells have been drilled for the new oilfield to go into regular production, the means must be ready to take the oil away. So the civil engineers will have

30 *View of a drilling rig during a Canadian winter*

been at work, laying pipelines and setting up storage tanks. They may also have had to lay roads to the well sites before any work could start at all. After all this engineering work has been done, the field should be able to produce oil with very few men in attendance. There will, of course, have to be some operators there to regulate flows from the wells, run the tank farms, pumps and other essential equipment, because without them the crude oil would never get to the refiners.

Old hands in refineries may tell you that all the world is divided into 'chemists' and 'engineers'. This is something of an exaggeration, but it expresses a fundamental truth. The people who direct operations on the process units, run the laboratory to check the quality of products, and plan production have often been trained as chemists, or perhaps as chemical engineers or physicists. The hour-by-hour operation of the plant and much of the bench-work in the laboratory is done by teams of people who do not have the same formal education, but their skills have been trained and developed so that they can do these essential parts of the refinery's work. On the way they will of necessity acquire a great deal of the special scientific knowledge which relates to oil.

The other 'half of the world' is equally essential to efficient refinery operation. The whole complex arrangement of process units, tank farms, power stations and produce loading areas depends utterly on the proper functioning of pumps, valves, measuring instruments and every kind of mechanical device. All these things must be kept in near-perfect condition to work continuously for months or years, with periodic checks and overhauls. So there must be a team of engineers, machine fitters, instrument mechanics, electricians, and many other engineering craftsmen to see that the machinery will do its job properly. A large refinery will also have its own building tradesmen, and like any other factory, it must have its own storemen, clerks, typists, etc.—some even have a shepherd with a flock of sheep to keep down the grass in the tank farm. Big refineries in remote parts of the world may have to run their own housing schemes and hospital, and all the social services which at home would be the responsibility of the local government.

Transportation of crude oil and products again involves a bewildering number of different kinds of worker. The biggest oil companies run tanker fleets of up to 100 vessels. Each ship requires manning, from the master, mate and chief engineer down to the cook's boy and the man who greases the propeller shaft. Even the small barge which plies up and down a big river to supply a local oil depot will have to have a crew. On land, the work of distributing oil requires depot operators who do similar work to those in the tank farm of a refinery. There must also be road tank car drivers, and an office organization to tell them where to go and what products they are to take. Deliveries by rail are left mainly to the professionals of the railways, but the oil company must still have engine drivers and shunters in its own depots and refineries.

All the larger oil companies have a research group. Its primary functions are to develop new products and processes, and to give advice and assistance to all other branches of the company and its customers on problems which cannot be tackled elsehwere for lack of people or special equipment. The staff of a research centre includes scientists of every description. There tends to be a predominance of chemists and physicists, but there must also be specialists in gological and engineering problems, statisticians and many others. These professional scientists, with their long and expensive training at university and on the job, are backed up by a large staff of technical and engineering assistants as well as the usual and most essential office and administrative staff.

No big firm, with such diversity of activities going on all over a country, or all over the world, can work efficiently without direction from the centre. Accordingly there must be a Head Office organization somewhere. The largest oil companies in the world are American and so have their headquarters in the United States. Among the giants are the Standard Oil Company of New Jersey (Exxon), Mobil Oil, the Texas Company, Standard Oil of California and the Gulf Oil Corporation. The two biggest non-American companies are Shell, which is part Dutch in origin and has what amounts to twin bases in London and The Hague, and British Petroleum (BP) which is run from London. Each of these companies has smaller off-shoots, or subsidiaries, in many other countries, with their own local headquarters. There are many other smaller companies, but they may still be very large concerns compared with other manufacturers and sellers of goods. The big ones usually enter into all the aspects of the oil business; the smaller ones sometimes concentrate on parts of the operation by, for instance, refining and selling oil, but buying their crude oil supplies from others.

One essential aspect of oil company headquarters work overflows to some extent into all the other operating departments and even to the more remote centres. This is oil supply planning, and for this a Supply Department is needed. The people who work in it need not be experts on oilfields or refining, or selling oil or navigating a tanker. But they must understand sufficient about each of these other jobs to assure that the best use is made of the company's resources. Many of the supply staff will have been trained as scientists, or mathematicians. Here, more even than in other departments, people cease to be specialists in particular branches of knowledge and become oil men.

In oil more than in most industries, success depends on the wise use of expensive equipment and advanced technol-

31   *A production platform in the North Sea*

ogy. There are large numbers of people in the work force who must have a professional scientific background. Many of the others who do not have this formal training must nevertheless be highly skilled in the use of the scientific and engineering techniques round which the modern industry is built. Much training must be done on the job, reinforced from time to time by special training courses. Despite all the computers and other advanced equipment, experience still counts for a great deal.

Most of the really large companies have operations in many countries. So far as possible, the local organizations will be staffed by local people because they know the language, and the ways in which governments and other commercial enterprises work. Such an arrangement is also usually cheaper for the employer. If an operation is to be started in an underdeveloped country, the position is rather different, because there will probably not be enough suitably educated and trained workers. So to begin with, while local people are being trained, a large part of the more senior staff and some of the lower ranks will have to be brought in from the company's headquarters and other centres. As the oilfield, or whatever operation is concerned, becomes established, local staff will increasingly take it over under guidance and direction from headquarters. There is continuous interchange of staff, permanent or visiting, between company centres, so that as many people as possible become familiar with the full scope of the company's work.

Day to day life in much of the oil industry is very like life anywhere else, but there are exceptions. Perhaps the most difficult life is that of the drillers in off-shore oil or gas-fields out at sea. They must live and work for two or three weeks at a time on their tiny man-made islands, in rather cramped quarters, with little time for relaxation, and no chance whatever of a change of scenery until the next relief crew

32 *At work on the drilling deck of exploration rig* Sea Quest

arrives. In addition to all the usual hazards of their kind of work, they must be prepared to face the dangers of storms and the extreme difficulties which may arise if something goes wrong in the well. There have been disasters from both causes, but no shortage of men who find this kind of life interesting, exciting and rewarding.

The one feature which distinguishes the oil industry from many others is that virtually all its operations go on twenty-four hours a day every day of the year. Drilling and the production of oil from the ground are continuous jobs, so are refining and the operation of tankers. Even office jobs are not untouched by the unceasing nature of the operations in the field. In some parts of an oil company it is always necessary to have a few people 'on call' at all hours of the day and night to help with emergencies or pass on instructions to or from remote corners of the world. If one wanted a motto for the industry's workers, it might well be 'We never close down'.

15 · Oil Today and Tomorrow

It is possible to view the year 1973 as a turning point in the history of the oil industry. The reasons are partly technical, but mainly economic and political, and these strands cannot be completely separated. Some of the changes were indeed starting to take shape earlier, though they had not been widely recognised. Events in 1973 made everyone aware that the future would show major changes for the whole industry and for all who are dependent on it in any way.

Over the years the Middle East oil states had been increasingly concerned to bring their oil fully under their own direct control. Politically, the concern is clear; no country likes to have its main resource owned and exploited by foreigners, in this case the oil companies which were mostly American or European in origin. Economically, the oil states had taken only limited steps to control prices and the rate of extraction of oil, and hence did not fully control the money coming in. Oil prices were increased in the early 1970's by raising tax and royalty rates charged by the member states of the Organisation of Petroleum Exporting Countries (OPEC) which includes the Middle East states, Venezuela and most of the African producers. There were also new moves towards the complete nationalisation of the oil companies' assets. At the end of 1973 pressure was intensified largely for a purely political reason—to influence those countries which had failed to support the Arabs in the latest round of their long-standing feud with Israel. The means adopted also affected all other countries, because prices were increased four-fold in the space of a few months, and production rates were heavily cut back.

Europe and Japan, which still import nearly all their oil, were in a state of crisis, with little liquid fuel available for any purpose. Consequently, there were reductions in all industrial activity as well as a degree of hardship for most people—since normal life for everyone depends at some point on oil fuels. At one time the U.S. used to be self-sufficient in oil, but in recent years has come to be dependent on imports for some 40 percent of its supplies, including much from the Arab states. For some months, it was forbidden for any Arab oil at all to be shipped to America, and the Eastern states in particular had a difficult winter. Slowly, through the next year, the embargoes were relaxed, and things returned to something like normal, except that world oil prices are still at levels which were unthinkable before 1973.

Grave economic damage was averted, because it is not in the ultimate interest of the producers to destroy the industry and livelihood of other nations. Nevertheless, no country can forget that the episode could be repeated, and that the high prices pose continued serious problems of how to raise money for essential oil supplies. Developing countries with none of their own oil are hardest hit, because they have most difficulty in increasing exports to pay for the oil they need. Without the oil, industry and much of agriculture can grind to a halt, exports become impossible, and all development stops.

Apart from the immediate political and economic effects, the oil crisis year of 1973-4 focused attention on a point which was previously often forgotten. Oil is an irreplaceable resource and there is not an unfailing supply available until the end of time, even barring political interference. If the rate of expansion of the 1950's and 1960's were to continue, and even assuming that new fields could be found at a reasonable rate, oil could start to become very scarce within less than fifty years. Such as can be found will be more and more difficult and expensive to exploit. The industry's best geologists consider it most unlikely that any large area of prolific fields such as those round the Persian Gulf will ever be found again. Even deposits the size of those in Alaska and the North Sea are something of a rarity. So, we must consider carefully how to make best use of the oil we have, and what other sources of energy can be developed.

The tar sands, oil shales and coal can be made to yield liquid fuels for transport and chemical feedstock—an obvious continuing job for the oil industry. The technology for making 'synthetic crude' needs much further development, but the price of the products will be increasingly competitive. The fundamentals of refining and distribution can be adapted to changes in kind and quantity of products, but there is need to plan a long way ahead and government, which should be taking a view of the long-term needs of all fuel producing and using industries, must assist in this process. In many countries, part of the energy supply industry, notably coal mining and electricity generation, is already in the hands of government; this in itself limits the scope for oil companies to widen their activities, without entering into the argument as to whether they already have too strong an economic position. Nevertheless, in the strictly technical field, the experience of the oil industry in geological exploration may still be of great use in the somewhat different conditions of an expanded search for coal and uranium.

An increasingly scarce and costly resource must not be used wastefully. There has to be a big drive to improve efficiency, prevent loss of heat from buildings and industrial processes, and ensure that low grade heat is put to work. More heat can be recovered from chimney flue gases and from the cooling water used in power stations and other industry.

Crude oil and gas must not be used in the future for jobs which can be done equally well by other energy sources. The emphasis must be on using oil products where nothing else will do, or where the alternatives will take a long time to develop.

For example, coal and nuclear power can replace oil and gas in electricity generation. Coal reserves are not unlimited either, but will last quite a lot longer than oil. Oil products will continue for some time to have an advantage in transportation of all kinds, but nuclear powered ships already exist, and electricity could replace diesel oil on many railways. Road transport is more of a problem, but the electric battery powered automobile and bus are already with us. Lightweight quick charging batteries would speed change in this area. It is particularly difficult to design aircraft to use anything other than petroleum fuels. Hydrogen made by the electrolysis of water is a possibility, and is completely non-polluting, but there are difficulties with safety and with the weight of the tanks to carry it. Chemicals and plastics now based on processing of petroleum distillates can also be made from coal.

The extent and timing of all changes is governed by the relative cost of various fuels. Conversion of existing equipment from oil to coal in power stations could be done fairly quickly, provided enough coal is available. An early effect on oil refining, which would be especially noticeable in Europe, could thus be a reduction in residual fuel oil compared to other products, with more conversion of residue and heavy distillates into lighter materials. Changes cannot be made quickly, since it takes at least three years to design and build a large refinery unit, even when a suitable process is ready for full-scale use. Also, conversion units require elaborate and expensive parts, and will themselves consume a great deal of energy in doing their work.

A further influence affects all aspects of production, transportation, refining and end-use of oil products—the effect on the environment. We have been made acutely aware in recent years of the undesirable effects of oil spills and other wastes in sea and rivers, of soot and sulphur dioxide in the air, and of possible long-term poisoning by the lead fluid used in motor gasoline. The oil industry and users of its products have made much progress towards limiting these unpleasant by-products of their activities.

In part this has been achieved voluntarily, in part under compulsion of the law. The technical means exist for making very substantial reductions in pollution, the problems lie partly in the cost. In the end, the consumer must pay, not only in cash, but also in the earlier use of energy resources which cannot readily be replaced, for the benefits of a better environment. Three examples illustrate this point very clearly.

Deliberate dumping of oily residues from tankers at sea has been much reduced, but only at the cost of carrying fairly large amounts of water around. Spills due to tankers going aground could be cut down, but this needs more elaborate and costly shipbuilding techniques and better navigational aids to keep them out of danger. Absolute safety in this respect would involve stopping tankers from plying the oceans and doing without oil from undersea wells. Such extreme measures are, in the end, unacceptable to most people. So we must work on improving the safety of oil operations at sea with the techniques we have, and keep the costs within limits which can be borne by oil users.

Desulphurisation of oil to reduce air pollution is already widely used, but at an increasing cost in process plants and use of refinery fuel. It is wasteful to insist on low sulphur fuels for users where no direct benefit can be shown to exist.

Low-lead gasoline is necessary to ensure the functioning of present designs of catalytic exhaust clean-up systems. Lead by itself, in the amounts given off by automobiles, is not a proven danger to health. Since the hazard is not accurately known, it is generally considered sensible to curb the unlimited use of lead fuel. Whatever the reasons and arguments for restricting the use of lead, there are problems of cost and energy conservation. With less lead in gasoline, lower octane numbers must be accepted, with lower engine efficiency and greater use of fuel. Alternatively, present quality can be maintained, but only by using larger amounts of useful oil fractions in the refinery at higher cost in money and resources.

In every case, if we are to protect both our environment and our long-term oil supplies, some compromise is necessary. At times the interests are in direct conflict. This is illustrated almost daily by the debates in Congress and wordy battles between the federal agencies responsible for environmental protection and energy planning.

Meantime, the day-to-day business of keeping everyone supplied with oil products must go on. The commercial structure of the industry is already starting to change under the influence of governments in both the producing and the consuming countries. Technical progress can and will be maintained, even though the day of the large company controlling its entire operation from the oil well to the consumer seems to be passing. Whoever controls it in the future, the industry as a whole still has much to contribute to economic and industrial progress for people all over the world.

Appendix: Oil Chemistry

In Chapter 5 we had a first look at the nature of oil. The chemistry of carbon compounds is a sufficient study to last several lifetimes, and we do not know the full story of all the substances which make up crude oils. But any reader who has started to learn some chemistry may find it interesting to have a brief introduction to the types of compound which have to be dealt with in analysing and processing petroleum. This section therefore goes into a little more detail than was possible in the main part of the book.

The simplest hydrocarbon is methane. It consists of one carbon atom, with four hydrogen atoms joined to it:

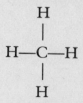

In chemist's shorthand we write this as CH_4. The nature of the methane molecule and the bulk properties of the substance have been known for a long time, since this is the explosive firedamp found in most coal mines. It is also the main constituent of the natural gas found under the North Sea. Methane is a gas under normal conditions, but it can be condensed by extreme cold to a liquid boiling at $-161°C$; it can also be condensed by applying a sufficiently high pressure.

Carbon atoms have the property that they must always form four links with other atoms in building up a compound. These links can be to other carbon atoms as well as to hydrogen or different elements. It is possible to build up chains of carbon atoms, filling up the spare links, or valencies, with hydrogen atoms. (Remember that molecules are very small and atoms even smaller, so that there are billions upon billions of molecules in a single gram of methane or anything else. We speak loosely about molecules in many instances where we are really concerned with the properties of a collection of countless millions of identical molecules.)

The next hydrocarbon of more elaborate structure than methane has two carbon atoms, one of the methane hydrogens having been replaced by a carbon with its own quota of hydrogen atoms. This compound is ethane, C_2H_6, or

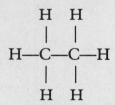

Ethane is also a gas, boiling at $-89°C$. We can carry on building up carbon chains in this manner to make the class of compounds known as paraffins. It is also possible to have branched chains of carbon atoms, and to have compounds in

which the carbons are linked to form a ring of five or six atoms. A special kind of ring compound, with less than the normal amount of hydrogen atoms, is benzene, and this is the first of the class called 'aromatics'.

$$
\begin{array}{c}
\text{C} \\
| \\
\text{C—C—C—C}
\end{array}
\qquad
\begin{array}{l}
\text{Branched chain} \\
\text{C}_5\text{H}_{12}
\end{array}
\qquad
\begin{array}{l}
\text{Iso-pentane} \\
\text{b.p. 28°C}
\end{array}
$$

$$
\begin{array}{c}
\text{C—C} \\
/ \qquad \backslash \\
\text{C} \qquad\quad \text{C} \\
\backslash \qquad / \\
\text{C—C}
\end{array}
\qquad
\begin{array}{l}
\text{Naphthene ring} \\
\text{C}_6\text{H}_{12}
\end{array}
\qquad
\begin{array}{l}
\text{Cyclo-hexane} \\
\text{b.p. 81°C}
\end{array}
$$

$$
\begin{array}{c}
\text{C=C} \\
/ \qquad \backslash \\
\text{C} \qquad\quad \text{C} \\
\backslash\backslash \qquad // \\
\text{C—C}
\end{array}
\qquad
\begin{array}{l}
\text{Aromatic ring} \\
\text{C}_6\text{H}_6
\end{array}
\qquad
\begin{array}{l}
\text{Benzene} \\
\text{b.p. 80°C}
\end{array}
$$

$$
\begin{array}{c}
\text{C=C} \\
/ \qquad \backslash \\
\text{C} \qquad\quad \text{C—C} \\
\backslash\backslash \qquad // \\
\text{C—C}
\end{array}
\qquad
\begin{array}{l}
\text{Aromatic ring+chain} \\
\text{C}_6\text{H}_5.\text{CH}_3
\end{array}
\qquad
\begin{array}{l}
\text{Toluene} \\
\text{b.p. 110°C}
\end{array}
$$

The carbon atom 'skeletons' of some simple hydrocarbon compounds are shown above. The hydrogen atoms have been left out to keep the diagram simple—in every case there must be a number of hydrogen atoms attached in such a way that each carbon has four links. Note the double links in the aromatic molecules. An important general rule is that for any particular class of compound—paraffin, naphthene or aromatic—the more carbon atoms are present the higher the boiling point will be.

The hydrocarbon gases, ethylene and propylene, have the same skeleton as ethane and propane, but each contains double-linked carbon atoms and fewer hydrogen atoms. Their formulae are C_2H_4 and C_3H_6. These and other similar compounds with four or more carbon atoms in their basic structure are called olefins; they are always more reactive than paraffins or the simple ring compounds.

The more complicated compounds in crude oil boil at temperatures up to about 1000°C, and so may be expected to have large molecules containing a considerable number of carbon atoms. Bearing in mind that crude oil consists of a mixture of hundreds or even thousands of different compounds, it will not be very surprising to find that any particular one is not likely to be present at more than 1 or 2 percent at most, and there may be much less. Also, the boiling points will be very close together, and if we boil a sample of crude oil it will show quite a smooth and steady increase in temperature as successively heavier compounds boil off.

In addition to the hydrocarbons there are small amounts of compounds containing other elements. The sulphur compounds are the most important, and sulphur may account for up to 2 or 3 percent of a crude oil. The sulphur compounds in crude oil contain one or more sulphur atoms built in chemically in a hydrocarbon chain or ring. There tends to be a higher proportion of sulphur among the higher-boiling parts of the crude oil. These compounds are generally objectionable. They are strong smelling, they tend to be corrosive, and when the oil is burnt they produce sulphur dioxide which is also smelly and corrosive. Crude oils may also contain small amounts of gas hydrogen sulphide, which smells like rotten eggs and is intensely poisonous. This, when found, is got rid of safely during refining so that we can have safe products which do not smell unpleasant.

The oxygen and nitrogen compounds are only present in very small amounts in most crude oils. The oxygen compounds tend to be slightly acidic; the nitrogen compounds are usually slightly basic or alkaline. Normally they are not present in sufficient quantity to need removal, but some crude oils contain enough to require special treatment in making particular products, where their special properties would be a nuisance.

Metallic compounds only occur in very small traces, and they are concentrated among the highest-boiling compounds in crude oil. For most purposes we can forget them, but if they are present in more than very minute quantities they may make difficulties in processing or in the final use of products. Oil refiners always have to be on the lookout for troubles of this kind, especially when working with a newly discovered type of crude oil for the first time.

Index